T H E
COLOUR AND
STYLE FILE

THE
COLOUR AND
STYLE FILE

BARBARA JACQUES

PIATKUS

© 1989 Barbara Jacques

First published in 1989 by
Judy Piatkus (Publishers) Limited
5 Windmill Street, London W1P 1HF

British Library Cataloguing in Publication Data

Jacques, Barbara
  The colour and style file
  1. Women's clothing. Selection – Manuals
  I. Title
  646′.34

  ISBN 0–86188–841–3
  ISBN 0–86188–899–5 (pbk)

Edited by Susan Fleming
Line illustrations by Eileen Graham
Photography by Ron Sutherland
Design by Sue Ryall

Typeset in Linotron Times by
Phoenix Photosetting, Chatham, Kent
Printed and bound in Great Britain by
Purnell Book Production Ltd, Paulton, Bristol

To women the world over, in the hope that this book
will help them to make the very best of themselves, and
be proud of their achievements.

To my father, who is always there when I need him.

To my two daughters – Terry and Vicki – and my son
Mitchell, and my grandchildren Dale, Rebecca,
Jonathan, Francesca and Christina who have brought much
joy into my life.

The Publishers wish to thank Alexon for the use of their colour photographs on page 114 and black and white photograph on page 14, and Dash for the use of their colour photographs on page 115. The Publishers also wish to thank Monet for loaning jewellery and artwork copied on pages 98 and 99, and Parks Dress Agency for the loan of clothes.
Hair by Anthony Yacomine at John Frieda, Make-Up by Gilda White (pages 22/3, 36, 39, 41, 43, 45, 47, 48, 113, 116).

The Publishers wish to point out that all colour reproduction in this book is subject to the limitations of the printing process.

ACKNOWLEDGEMENTS

A book like this doesn't just happen, it is a combination of the talents and experiences of many different people. First, to my publishers and to Philip Cotterell who at frequent intervals over the past five years has encouraged me to write *The Colour and Style File*. His faith in my ability has never wavered and I will always be eternally gratefully to him for his encouragement. To Judy Piatkus for her enthusiasm for the book. To Gill Cormode for her foresight, dedication and the professional way in which she directed the preparation of the book. To Susan Mears for her dedication, understanding and her calming influence as well as her talent in bringing the book to life. To Susan Fleming whose help in restructuring was invaluable as was her home cooking which I appreciated during the long sessions we spent together.

To my husband Brian for the love and devotion he lavishes on me plus all the help and support he gave me to get the book on the road.

To Carole Jackson, author of *Colour Me Beautiful* for showing me other ways to develop my talents and for her continual friendship.

To Doris Pooser, author of *Always in Style* for our continual exchange of ideas which have helped us both to grow as well as the industry around us.

To Avis Charles of Parks Dress Agency for her creativity as well as for loaning clothes from her nearly new designer collection which have been used by some of the models in the book. To Stewart Mechem, Alison Cook and Karen Smith from Alexon for their help and support and for the use of Alexon clothes for some of the models, and for their colour transparencies. To Debbie Hugill from Dash for supplying some of their colour transparencies and Penny Briers from Monet for her co-operation and the use of some beautiful Monet jewellery worn by the models.

To Gilda White for her make-up artistry. To my hairdresser – Anthony Yacomine from John Frieda for his creative talents with which he created sheer magic. To the models who appear in the book for giving of their time and patience – Vanessa Charles, Julia Eccles, Pauline Crawford, Anne Ponsonby, Susan Mears, Susie Davis, Lisa del Rosso, Lynne Williams, Wei San and Jane Bewick.

To all the trainers from The Academy of Colour and Style (International) Ltd for their loyal support and help – especially Brenda Jennings and Pauline Crawford for their exchange of ideas and talents. To all the Academy's consultants who are working and showing women from all over the world how to make the most of themselves.

CONTENTS

*I*NTRODUCTION

Have you noticed how some people seem to have the knack of being able to pick an item of clothing off a rail, and instinctively know the style and the colour will be right for them? They also know how to mix and match other items and accessories with that new article of clothing to create a variety of interesting and exciting looks. Infuriating isn't it?

Those of us without such talent tend to excuse our less inspiring appearance with the comment that these lucky people have been born with the gift, because they are naturally creative or have natural flair. Now, this may be true in some cases, but above all, the secret of their success is that they know *themselves:* their best colours and their bodies; they know what lines of clothing suit them best; and they know how to work with and develop fashion to suit their own particular lifestyle and image.

Even if you think you'll never have this talent, don't despair, you *can* learn the 'rules'. I am here to help you – just follow my advice in *The Colour and Style File*. My book will take you through everything you need to know to help you create your own individual clothes style. Instead of battling with a wardrobe full of haphazard purchases, you will learn how to make your wardrobe work for you, and develop a unique and confident style.

■ Step One: Colour

The most important thing this book will teach you is an awareness and understanding of colour and its effects. I became intrigued by colour and what colour could do for people more than 35 years ago, when I worked as the colour coordinator for my family's interior design business. Working with colour in the home, I became fascinated by the many 'moods' of colour, and how these moods could be used to help lift the spirits or calm and soothe, to create a warm friendly atmosphere or even a cool and remote feel. I would study closely the lifestyle of people whose homes we were re-modelling before I put forward our recommendations for a total transformation.

But my greatest fulfilment came after I had left the interior design business (having developed an allergic asthma because of the wallpaper and dust). My change of direction took me into colour cosmetics and colour coordination. Working in the cosmetics field really brought home to me how the clever use of colour can change people's lives. I will never forget some of the *personal* transformations and, even more important, the tremendous changes of attitude which were brought about when a little imagination was used. It was remarkable to see how a woman who thought she was plain and unattractive suddenly became interested in and positive about her looks when we used the right shades of make-up to bring out her natural beauty. By learning which colours suit *you* best (for we're all different), and seeing how to coordinate these best colours, you can transform yourself and your life too.

▉ Step Two: Figure Image

The next step involves recognising your own figure image. We all have different face shapes and body shapes, and various good and bad points. This is what makes each one of us unique.

Instead of despairing about the bad points – which so many of us do – you can, by recognising and *admitting* them, learn how to camouflage them. I have seen so many negative women who felt they were complete failures because of their bodies; they thought they could never look good because they were too small, or tall, or skinny, or thought that being fat meant being ugly. All had, one way or another, given up on themselves, using this as an excuse. But remember, most of us do have very positive points – for instance, a lot of plump girls have very good legs or skin – and we must all learn how to bring people's attention to these. I have spent the last 22 years helping small women feel tall, tall women feel proud, and fat women feel beautiful. Most importantly, I have helped them change their attitudes about themselves, encouraging them to make the most of what they have got, with fantastic results.

Looking good has nothing to do with weight or height – the secret of success lies in the art of visual balance. Stay with me, and I'll tell you all about it! The second part of my book will get you to look at yourself *very* closely and critically, completely without any self-deception – this may well be the most difficult lesson for you to learn!

■ Step Three: Clothing Lines

The third step is learning how to choose the lines in clothes that suit you best. For instance, a 'straight' person (one of the many figure types that I define), will look better in straight lines – tailored shirts, skirts and jackets, square and boat necks – than in clothes which are rounded and softer looking in cut. This part of the book uses basic illustrations and a unique numbering identification system which, once you know how to use it (and it's really very easy), will enable you, virtually at a glance, to recognise your own best styles in jewellery and handbags! This, plus all the other knowledge you will acquire, will turn shopping trips from a nightmare of frustration to a dream!

■ Co-ordinated Wardrobe

Your fourth and final step is learning how to put all your newly acquired knowledge and enthusiasm into practice. A wardrobe that works for you is based on mixing and matching items of clothing which harmonise in colour, fabric and cut; if you follow my simple instructions you should immediately be able to look afresh at what you already have, and buy new items with a keener, more discriminating and more informed eye.

■ The New, Confident You

Above all, the most important thing *The Colour and Style File* can give you is confidence. Self-assurance is your key to success at work and at home, and once you feel secure in the knowledge that you are looking your best you are sure to make progress. Remember, success breeds success! You, too, can be beautiful and unique and possess that indefinable quality of chic which you have admired in others. *The Colour and Style File* will show you how!

I sincerely hope that reading and following my advice in this book will open your eyes to the wonderful world of colour and shape around you, to the beauty of *you* – and to the self-fulfilment and contentment that being at ease and in harmony with oneself and one's surroundings can bring.

Barbara Jacques

*A co-ordinated look which feels right will bring
self-assurance and poise.*

PART ONE

*C*OLOUR

*C*ONFIDENCE

Have you ever considered the importance of colour to you? It can affect your mood, your body shape, your perspective on life, and the overall impression you make on others. Colour has an immediate and powerful influence on us all, often affecting us without our realising it, yet our *use* of colour – in the clothes we wear, and the colours we use in our homes – is often a sadly hit-and-miss affair.

Reading this book will give you an understanding of the basic rules of colour, and will provide you with a tool which enables you to alter perception, shape or mood, to stimulate the imagination, or to provide tranquillity. You will learn where colour comes from, and how one colour can influence and change another colour, when placed alongside it. Then you'll realise how a knowledge of colour relationships can help you achieve success in colour coordination so you can wear any colour, and you'll discover how to use colour to your advantage and adapt it to your unique requirements.

I can promise you that the time you spend understanding colour will be repaid over and over again, as you see colour anew, become more aware of its potential, and learn how to handle it with confidence. You will learn to use colour in a way that expresses your individuality and gives you a strong and positive self-image. You might not trust your own instincts on colour because usually you made mistakes in the past. But why was this? Simply because you either never took the time to learn the simple basics, or you had your instinctive choices challenged by others and had their opinions forced upon you. Before we go any further, you must try to throw away the years of conditioning and get back to your individual perspective on colour. Then you can start to build the new, colour-confident you!

The Main Characteristics of Colour

It's really easy to gain confidence in colour. You just need to learn the basic rules, and to practise working with them. As you know, confidence comes from 'doing', so let's start with a little test to find out what you actually *see*. Look at the page opposite and describe simply and quickly what you see by filling in the blanks.

If you got *light* blue and *dark* blue for 1., *bright* red and *muted* or *toned-down* red for 2., *yellow* green and *blue* green for 3., well done – you came up with the three main characteristics of colour.

The characteristics are as follows:

1. *Intensity*   How *dark* or how *light*?
2. *Clarity*   How *bright* or how *muted*?
3. *Undertone*   How *warm* or how *cool*?

INTENSITY: DARK

At its simplest, *intensity dark* includes all colours where you have to put the word 'dark' before the colour to describe it properly. For example, dark is the main characteristic of the following colours – dark blue, dark brown, dark green and so on.

INTENSITY: LIGHT

The term *intensity light* includes all colours where you have to put the word 'light' before the colour, as light is the main characteristic of the colour. This could include for example, light blue, light pink, light aqua, light green, light yellow, light brown and so on.

CLARITY: BRIGHT

Reduced to its simplest, bright or clear clarity includes all colours where very little or no undertone can be seen, where you have to put the word 'bright' before the colour, bright being its main characteristic – for example, bright true red, bright blue, and bright turquoise.

CLARITY: MUTED

This includes all colours before which you have to use the word 'muted' or a word which suggests toned-down. Muted or toned-down is the main characteristic of the colour – for example, muted red, grey navy, grey green and so on.

UNDERTONE: WARM

At its simplest, this includes all colours before which you would use a word which suggests warmth, in other words sufficient yellow has been added to change the temperature to warm, and warm is now the main characteristic of the colour – for example, warm green, warm blue, warm pink, warm or orangey red and so on.

UNDERTONE: COOL

This includes all colours where sufficient blue has been added to the true colour to change its natural name from, say, green to blue green, and the temperature to cool, cool being the main characteristic of the colour – for example, blue red and blue green.

So now you know how to look at colours. Simple, isn't it!

As your eye becomes more accustomed to looking at different colours, you will discover that all colours where warm or cool is the main characteristic will be of medium intensity. As the colour starts to go darker, the undertone becomes much less apparent, and the deepness or darkness of the colour will become the first characteristic. The same rule applies to light colours: as the colours start to become light, the undertone will take second place to the lightness. The lightness then becomes the first characteristic and the undertone becomes the second, less important, characteristic.

THE COLOUR TEST

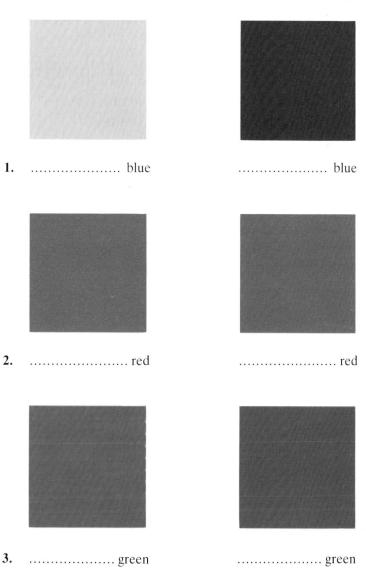

1. .... blue   .... blue

2. .... red   .... red

3. .... green   .... green

The Colour Wheel

The colour wheel is an easy and simple way of helping you understand where all colours come from, how colour is built up, and how colours relate and react to one another.

Now study the colour wheel opposite. Look first at the three *primary* colours – red, blue and yellow. The colours are pure, clear, and *true* (which is what primary means here), and these three colours are the source of *all* the colour we see. This is because all other colours are derived, or 'mixed' from them. The three *secondary* colours situated equally between the primary colours – violet, green and orange – are created by mixing equal parts of each of the primary colours on either side of them on the colour wheel.

Also, the wheel can help us to understand other things about colour too. As you can see, the primary colours of red, blue and yellow do not have an undertone – they are *true* with no admixture – but they do have a *feeling* (which is different to undertone). By closing your eyes and thinking of the colours individually, you will discover they convey a warm or cool feeling: red gives a feeling of warmth (like fire) as does yellow (like sunshine); but blue gives a feeling of coolness (like water). Because these three colours are bright and clear, with no undertone, their first colour characteristic is *bright*.

Next look at two of the secondary colours, violet and green. You will see that they are a mixture of equal parts of a warm and a cool feeling colour. This is why when you try to visualise these two colours you will experience some conflict regarding their 'feel' (is it warm or cool?). This is because they are neither. In fact both cancel each other out. Therefore, you should consider them as still belonging to the bright palette, they are bright with no undertone. The third secondary colour is quite different.

When you mix red and yellow together, two warm-feeling colours, to make orange, this now becomes a warm *undertone* instead of just a warm-feeling colour, and therefore orange has *warm* as its first colour characteristic.

By studying the primary and other colour wheels, and the various colour fans in the following pages, you will be able to see quite clearly the many ways in which colours relate to each other.

RELATED COLOURS

I use this term to describe colours which are close to each other on the wheel, and which have been used in each other's mixing. For example, blue is a blood relative, you might say, of green and violet, because 50 per cent of their mix was blue; and red is a blood relative of orange and violet, as yellow is of orange and green and so on. It can be compared to a blood or half brother/sister relationship. Other related colours are various shades of the one colour, also called monochromatic colours.

Related colours can be used happily together in coordination or combination.

COMPLEMENTARY COLOURS

This term describes colours which are opposite one another on the colour wheel, neither of which has been used in the making of the other. So, red is opposite green, blue is opposite orange, and yellow is opposite violet.

You will find that adding a small amount of a complementary colour to an outfit or colour scheme can lift it and make it come to life.

COLOUR WHEEL SHOWING PRIMARY AND SECONDARY COLOURS

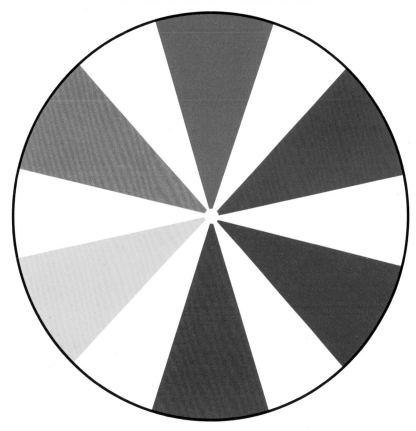

(Clockwise from top) *Primary Red, Secondary Violet, Primary Blue, Secondary Green, Primary Yellow, Secondary Orange*

NEUTRAL COLOURS

These do not appear on the colour wheel. However, imagine that you are an artist, and that you mixed the three primary colours, red, blue and yellow together. The result would be that you would neutralise them, making them into a grey. This is not a colour in the true sense; neither is black, white or any colour approaching grey, black or white. For example, olive is a grey green and near to grey; pine green is close to black, as is navy blue; off white and beiges are close to white. Camel to dark brown colours are also considered neutrals; mahogany, for instance, is really a red grey.

Other neutrals come from mixing two complementary colours together: as they become low in colour or saturation, approaching grey or a nondescript colour, the combination becomes a neutral, one colour neutralising the other.

THE SIX COLOUR WHEELS

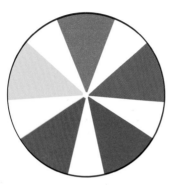

Bright (clockwise from top) *True Red, Medium Violet, True Blue, True Green, Bright Yellow*

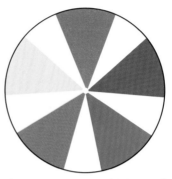

Light (clockwise from top) *Watermelon Red, Light Violet, Medium Blue, Medium Blue Green, Light Lemon Yellow*

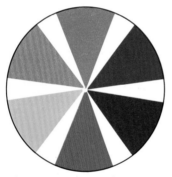

Warm (clockwise from top) *Bright Orange Red, Warm Purple, Marine Navy, Bright Yellow Green, Gold, Orange*

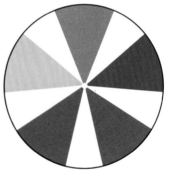

Muted (clockwise from top) *Watermelon Red, Muted Purple, Medium Grey Blue, Olive, Gold*

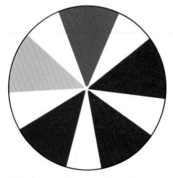

Dark (clockwise from top) *Bright Burgundy, Royal Purple, Navy, Forest Green, Yellow Gold*

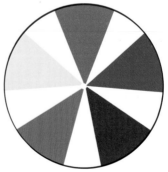

Cool (clockwise from top) *Blue Red, Plum, Grey Navy, Deep Blue Green, Lemon Yellow*

Colour and you

Now that you have learned how to recognise the different characteristics of colour in general, and where colour comes from, I want to teach you how to recognise your own natural colouring, in your hair, eyes and skin.

After years of research and testing many different methods of colour analysis on literally thousands of people, I developed what I call my *tonal concept*. This is not only the most accurate way of analysis, but the formula I worked out is also very simple to learn and to work with. This is because the concept is based on colour in its purest form, as are people themselves. By this, I mean that everybody has a major colour characteristic or look, a first impression, that can be fairly easily identified. There are six of these major or first characteristics, and they correspond to the six general characteristics of colour that I have already defined – dark, light, bright, muted, warm or cool. Thus, immediately, we have *six* different types of individual colouring.

Also, a person will often have admixtures of *other* tones which make the first dominant characteristic more individual. For example, in my tonal concept, a 'dark' person can have secondary characteristics of 'bright' or 'muted'; and a muted person can have secondary characteristics of 'dark' or 'light'. This is what gives us our uniqueness.

■ Your First Characteristic

So, let's now try to recognise your first most dominant characteristic. Look in a mirror. What do you see first? Do you see yourself as dark or light, bright or muted, warm or cool? Whichever it is, that is your *first* characteristic. Looking at the photographs overleaf might help too; do you have similar colouring to any of the girls?

■ Your Second Characteristic

Next, you can move on to find your second characteristic. Identifying both characteristics, primary and secondary, will enable you to recognise and understand your own uniqueness, and see how to wear your colours in your most individual and creative way.

Just like the colours we have been studying, some people can have variable amounts of light or dark, clear or muted and warm or cool, which can be their first characteristic. It is these numerous combinations that make us so individual, balance and harmony result when you wear colours that have the same or similar characteristics as your own personal colouring.

■ Which Tonal Group Are You?

In the following pages I have defined the six main characteristics of my tonal concept. I explain to you how to identify which basic type you are, define your main tonal fan colours – the ones you will look *best* in – and help you identify your secondary characteristic along with its colours which, when used in combination with your main fan colours, will give you your unique look. In these main fan colours we include some neutrals, and at the side of the page are the neutrals all the colour groups can wear. There are some further hints about wearing neutrals on pages 37–50.

Once you have read through all the following descriptions, you will have found your main characteristic and will be wanting to confirm it. Or perhaps you will have eliminated most of the colour characteristics which are *not* you, and you could be dithering between two.

RECOGNISING YOUR TONAL GROUP

Do you see **bright** first?

Do you see **dark** first?

Do you see **muted** first?

Do you see **muted** first?

Do you see **warm** first?

Do you see **light** first?

Do you see **dark** first?

Do you see **warm** first?

Do you see **cool** first?

So, how can you be sure you've got it right? Simple, go back over all the colour wheels and fans, discount the ones you have eliminated, and just concentrate on the ones you are left with. Then look in your wardrobe, your friends' wardrobes, or a fabric store, and match up the reds, blues and greens from the coloured fans you are working with. (We use the green in place of yellow as this shows more clearly). Drape one shoulder with one red, and the other with the other red, and compare the two. Which is best? Which harmonises with you, or are they both good? Do the same with the blues and the greens. This is the way you should always compare colour, by testing one shade of colour against another – *together*. Viewing one colour at a time is not an accurate way to drape and test, as the eyes do not change quickly enough and your brain can start to play tricks, only seeing what it wants to see. Neither can your memory keep up with all the changes.

Once you have found which colour fan looks best for you, you have found your main characteristic of colour. Then, using the same methods, find your second colour characteristic. You will now find that you can wear all the colours from your first and second characteristics, including all the colours *in between* the two fans, giving you a fantastically wide range of colours. These will all help to make you realise that you really are unique, and instead of being a fraught experience accompanied by costly mistakes, shopping will become a pleasure as you discover the wide range of colours you can wear.

So, recognising the family of colours in which your body's neutral, complementary and accent colours can be found, is the first step to colour appreciation. Let us take a look at the main characteristics of colour again, this time relating them to the individual.

(From left to right, starting at top) *Susan first characteristic Bright, second characteristic Dark; Pauline first characteristic Dark, second characteristic Bright; Vanessa Dark; Susie Muted; Jane first characteristic Muted, second characteristic Dark; Anne first characteristic Warm, second characteristic Light; Wei San first characteristic Warm, second characteristic Dark; Julia first characteristic Light, second characteristic Bright; Lynne first characteristic Cool, second characteristic Light.*

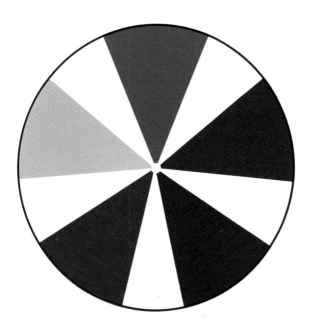

Dark Colour Wheel

Skin: deep brown, rose brown, mahogany, bronze, blue black
Eyes: brown, red brown, black brown, black

Asian colouring
Hair: dark brown, chestnut, black brown, black, blue black
Skin: beige, olive, bronze
Eyes: red brown, brown black, grey black, black

Oriental colouring
Hair: dark brown, black brown, black, blue black
Skin: ivory, beige olive, bronze
Eyes: dark brown, grey black, black, hazel grey

DARK TONAL GROUP

When dark is your first characteristic, people will notice your deep exotic colouring first. You will have dark hair, dark eyes, and you will already know that you look good in dark colours.

Vanessa (see page 23) is a Dark, with no secondary characteristic, but Pauline (page 22) has bright as her secondary characteristic and will look good in colours from both colour fans.

Caucasian colouring
Hair: dark brown to black, chestnut to auburn
Skin: ivory, beige, olive or bronze
Eyes: dark grey, deep olive, deep hazel or dark brown

Black colouring
Hair: brown, black-brown, blue black

▉ Dark-Bright

When your second characteristic is bright, you have a dark-bright look. You will have more contrast between your skin and hair than a dark-muted – a little like Snow-White with brown or very dark eyes. You can take a greater contrast with your colours, and you need to coordinate your dark to medium neutrals with bright colours. You will be able to wear a strong contrast like black and white, but this look would benefit from the addition of a bright scarf, handkerchief, flower, belt or jewellery to give it life and bring it in line with your body's natural colouring.

▉ Dark-Muted

When muted is your second characteristic, you will have a warm-looking eye or a warm look about your dark hair or skin. If this is you, you should accessorise your dark colours with medium to dark colours that are slightly warm. The contrasts will not be as strong as the dark-bright person, but let your body be your guide as to how muted and how big a contrast you should be aiming for.

Dark Fan

(From left to right)
True Red
Mahogany
Royal Purple
Dark Periwinkle Blue
True Blue
Teal Blue
Pine Green
Forest Green
Olive Green
Yellow Gold

Dark Bright

(From left to right)
Deep Hot Pink
Magenta
Shocking Pink
Bright Burgundy
Medium Violet
Royal Blue
Chinese Blue
True Green
Emerald Green
Bright Yellow

Dark Muted

(From left to right)
Pumpkin
Rust
Dark Tomato Red
Muted Purple
Marine Navy
Terracotta
Turquoise
Moss Green
Coffee Brown
Warm Beige

Neutrals for all dark tonal groups

(From left to right) *Oyster White, Grey Beige, Light True Grey, Medium True Grey, Charcoal Grey, Dark Chocolate Brown, Navy, Black.*

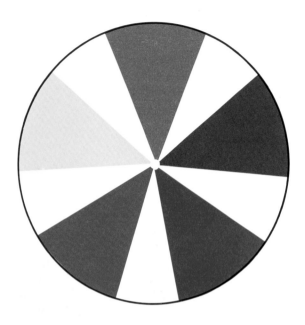

Light Colour Wheel

LIGHT TONAL GROUP

When light is your first characteristic, it will be your light appearance which will be noticed first. Words like 'delicate', 'fair', 'pale' and 'fragile' could be used to describe your overall look which will be light to medium intensity, with little contrast between hair and skin. You can have slightly warm or cool undertones.

Julia (see page 22) has light as her first characteristic and bright as her second. She looks good in colours from both colour fans.

Caucasian colouring
Hair: naturally golden or ash blonde, ranging from very light to medium light ash to light brown
Skin: from ivory to beige, and can have a pink or peach tone

Eyes: not deep, from light blue to blue-grey and aqua

Black colouring
Hair: light to black brown, red brown to ash brown with a soft look
Skin: rose beige to deep rose, camel brown to cocoa
Eyes: rose brown, brown to brown black

Asian colouring
Hair: ash brown, brown to brown black, with a soft look
Skin: pale ivory pink or beige to rose beige
Eyes: rose brown, brown black, grey black

Oriental colouring
Hair: ash brown, brown black, ash black
Skin: pink beige, rose beige, ivory beige, clear beige
Eyes: grey brown, brown black, ash black

■ Light-Bright

When bright is your second characteristic, there will be some apparent brightness about your eyes and skin, giving you a light-bright effect. You will find that bright colours bring you to life, although too much might be overpowering. You might have to be careful not to wear two light colours together, unless you can accessorise with a bright scarf, handkerchief, belt or jewellery to give the combination life and bring it in line with your body's natural look.

■ Light-Muted

When muted is your second characteristic giving you a light greyed-down effect, you will find the bright and dark colours too overpowering. At the opposite extreme, if a colour is *too* muted, it will look muddy and drab. Your body colours are a guide to how strong and muted your darker colours should be. Above all, the colours you wear have to bear a relationship with your body's natural colour in undertone, intensity and clarity.

Light Fan

(From left to right)
Pastel Pink
Clear Salmon
Deep Rose
Water Melon Red
Medium Violet
Medium Blue
Powder Blue
Light Blue Green
Light Lemon Yellow
Light Blue Grey

Light Muted

(From left to right)
Powder Pink
Orchid
Mauve
Rose Pink
Rose Beige
Pastel Blue Green
Deep Blue Green
Pastel Aqua
Sky Blue
Grey Blue

Light Bright

(From left to right)
Warm Pastel Pink
Coral Pink
Clear Bright Pink
Clear Bright Red
Golden Tan
Periwinkle Blue
Light Clear Gold
Light Aqua
Peach
Buff

Neutrals for all light tonal groups

(From left to right) *Soft White, Ivory, Light Beige, Light Warm Grey, Light Camel, Cocoa, Charcoal Blue Grey, Grey Navy*

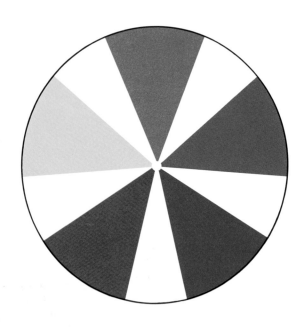

Bright Colour Wheel

Caucasian colouring

Hair: medium to dark in intensity from brown to black, ash to golden

Skin: light, ivory, beige, porcelain, and can look translucent with no apparent undertone

Eyes: blue, green, turquoise, steel grey

Black colouring

Hair: ash brown, deep brown, black-brown, black

Skin: deep beige, cocoa, light creamy brown

Eyes: brown-black, black

Asian colouring

Hair: dark brown, black brown, black

Skin: ivory, porcelain

Eyes: brown-black, black

Oriental colouring

Hair: black, dark brown

Skin: ivory, porcelain, bright

Eyes: black, brown black

BRIGHT TONAL GROUP

When bright is your first characteristic, it will not only be the brightness which will grab your attention, but you will have hair which is dark in comparison to your skin tone, giving an obvious contrast. Whatever colour your eyes are, they will be bright and jewel-like.

A true bright should always strive to stay snappy. You wear your clear bright colours to emphasise the bright radiance of your natural colouring. Muted, powdery or dull tones are not best for you. If you have any in your wardrobe, use one of your best bright colours which is a relative or complementary colour in a bright clarity as an accent to bring it more in line with your body's natural look. Susan (see page 22) is bright first and dark second. Contrast her colouring with Pauline, who is dark first and bright second.

■ Bright-Dark

When dark is your second characteristic, giving you a bright-dark look, you should always try to achieve contrast. How bright and how dark will be determined by the depth of colour of your hair, the lightness of your skin, and intensity (the darkness as opposed to lightness) of your eyes. The depth of brightness will vary in individuals, and the depth of hair and eyes will generally determine how deep a colour you can wear. Bright-dark types should be careful when wearing two lights together; adding a dark or bright accent near the face will help.

■ Bright-Light

When light is your second characteristic, you will have medium to light eyes, more prominent in colour and effect than those of bright-darks. Dark colours with brights are not your best look, but by adding a light accent near your face, you will make the dark-bright combination wearable for you.

Bright Fan

(From left to right)
Shocking Pink
Clear Bright Pink
True Red
Medium Violet
Deep Periwinkle Blue
True Blue
Chinese Blue
Hot Turquoise
True Green
Bright Yellow

Bright Light

(From left to right)
Peach
Clear Salmon
Bright Coral
Clear Bright Red
Emerald Turquoise
Light True Blue
Light Clear Navy
Clear Bright Aqua
Light Clear Gold
Light Warm Grey

Bright Dark

(From left to right)
Deep Hot Pink
Magenta
Blue Red
Bright Burgundy
Royal Purple
Royal Blue
Light True Green
Emerald Green
Lemon Yellow
Black

Neutrals for all bright tonal groups

(From left to right) *White, Soft White, Ivory, Grey Beige, Light True Grey, Medium True Grey, Charcoal Grey, Navy*

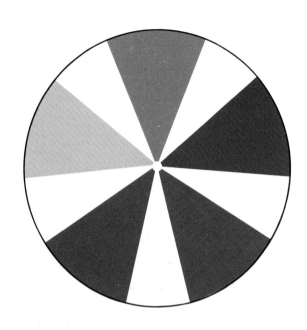

Muted Colour Wheel

MUTED TONAL GROUP

When muted is your first characteristic, you can seem to have unrelated groups of body colours, such as dark brown eyes, blonde hair and golden taupe skin, or warm hair and cool skin which is medium in intensity with a softness. At the same time there can be an impression of strength around the jawline, which can sometimes look darker in colour than the rest of the face. The deeper the skin tone, the fairer the hair and eyes can seem to be.

Toned-down colours look striking with your muted colouring, and light to medium mixes of your best neutrals look stunning. Bright and intense clarities can look harsh and garish. You can combine almost everything in your palette except extremes: medium and soft levels of contrast are the appropriate looks for you.

Susie (see page 22) is a Muted, and Jane is a Muted/Dark. Can you see the difference between the two?

Caucasian colouring
Hair: usually medium to dark blonde or a mix of both, ash or golden, medium brown
Skin: ivory, beige, golden to bronze
Eyes: medium to dark, hazel, green, green blue, medium to dark brown

Black colouring
Hair: ash brown, brown to black brown
Skin: beige to light brown, cocoa to rose brown
Eyes: hazel, rose brown, brown black, grey brown

Asian colouring
Hair: brown to ash brown, rose brown to mahogany, soft black
Skin: beige to red beige, bronze
Eyes: hazel, rose brown to grey brown, to black brown

Oriental colouring
Hair: mahogany, grey brown, brown, ash black
Skin: beige, pink beige, red beige (can have stronger pigmentation around jawline)
Eyes: hazel brown, hazel green, rose brown, grey brown, brown, black brown

■ Muted-Dark

When your second characteristic is dark, you will have a warm look about your eyes. Hazel eyes are the most common, warm because of the yellow in them. Your skin also can have a warm look to it.

■ Muted-Light

When your second characteristic is light, you will actually see, for instance, a beige colour rather than a warmth to the skin, which has very little colour and will need blusher. But you could have warmish skin and eyes, along with ash blonde hair which dictates the cool look. Muted-cools are a mixture of contradictions!

Muted Fan

(From left to right)
Deep Apricot
Watermelon Red
Muted Burgundy
Muted Purple
Grey Navy
Jade Green
Olive Green
Rose Brown
Green Grey
Gold

Muted Dark

(From left to right)
Salmon
Bittersweet
Warm Purple
Mahogany
Dark Chocolate Brown
Moss Green
Forest Green
Teal Blue
Autumn Grey
Camel

Muted Light

(From left to right)
Rose Pink
Mauve
Deep Rose
Light Periwinkle Blue
Medium Blue Grey
Deep Blue Green
Medium Blue Green
Light Lemon Yellow
Powder Blue
Light Blue Grey

Neutrals for all muted tonal groups

(From left to right) *Soft White, Oyster White, Rose Beige, Grey Beige, Cocoa, Coffee Brown, Charcoal Blue Grey, Marine Navy*

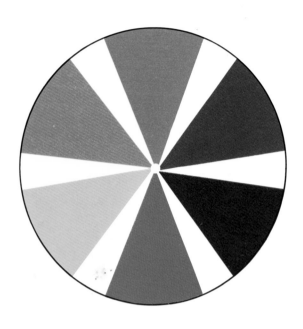

Warm Colour Wheel

WARM TONAL GROUP

When warm is your first characteristic, it will be quite apparent from the golden glow which will surround you. You will be of medium intensity, but if your hair or eyes are darker than medium intensity, you will find you will be able to add darker colours in stripes and accents. Your hair, eyes and skin will all radiate warmth.

Anne (see page 23) is a Warm/Light and Wei San (see page 22) is a Warm/Dark.

Caucasian colouring
Hair: golden to strawberry blonde with warm highlights
Skin: ivory, golden beige to bronze, freckles
Eyes: brown, taupe, green, hazel, blue-green with golden sunbursts

Black colouring
Hair: golden brown, brown with warmth, chestnut and brown-black

Skin: light golden brown and creamy brown to golden brown, bronze to mahogany, freckles
Eyes: hazel, topaz, warm brown to deep brown

Asian colouring
Hair: golden brown, dark brown, auburn to chestnut
Skin: ivory, golden beige, bronze, freckles
Eyes: hazel, topaz, warm brown, deep brown to brown-black

Oriental colouring
Hair: golden brown, chestnut, dark brown
Skin: golden beige, bronze
Eyes: warm brown, hazel, green hazel, brown hazel, deep brown, topaz

■ Warm-Light

When light is your second characteristic, your skin will be clear and light. When choosing your colours, think slightly warm undertones first, with a clear light to bright intensity. Depending on how bright your look is, many warm-lights can accessorise with the light true colours.

■ Warm-Dark

When dark is your second characteristic, you are a warm-based person with medium to strong warm colouring, usually very warm-looking eyes, and with a burnished look to your hair. The skin is of light to medium intensity, with a grey or brownish look about the jawline. The warm-dark types do not take bright strong colours or contrast well. Slightly warm toned-down colours are best.

Warm Fan

(From left to right)
Peach
Salmon
Bright Orange
Rust
Medium Golden Brown
Yellow Gold
Bright Yellow Green
Turquoise
Teal Blue
Warm Purple

Warm Light

(From left to right)
Light Apricot
Bright Coral
Orange
Orange Red
Light Clear Gold
Golden Tan
Clear Bright Aqua
Lime Green
Emerald Turquoise
Dark Periwinkle Blue

Warm Dark

(From left to right)
Pumpkin
Terracotta
Mahogany
Medium Bronze
Dark Chocolate Brown
Olive Green
Forest Green
Dark Periwinkle
Muted Purple
Dark Tomato Red

Neutrals for all warm tonal groups

(From left to right) *Soft White, Ivory, Buff, Warm Beige, Camel, Coffee, Autumn Grey, Marine Navy*

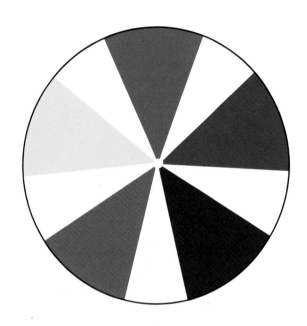

Cool Colour Wheel

COOL TONAL GROUP

When cool is your first characteristic, you will have medium intensity with a slight soft look, cool-looking eyes and skin. As a totally cool-looking person you are quite unique – there aren't many of you around. However, as we get older, we can become cooler looking as our hair greys, losing its pigmentation. The greyer your hair, the cooler you will be. A blue undertone has a toning-down effect on any colour, and you can see this when you compare the cool fan with the cool-dark fan.

   Lynne (on page 23) is a Cool, and her secondary characteristic is Light.

Caucasian colouring
Hair: ash blonde, grey dark blonde to dark brown
Skin: beige, pink, rose beige, and can be sallow
Eyes: cool, grey blue, blue green, rose brown, grey brown

Black colouring
Hair: ash brown, blue black, black, grey
Skin: rose brown, cocoa to dark brown, grey brown, blue black
Eyes: rose brown, grey brown, black brown

Asian colouring
Hair: dark brown, chestnut, brown black, blue black, grey
Skin: pink, rose beige, grey beige
Eyes: rose brown, grey brown, black brown

Oriental colouring
Hair: blue black, brown black, dark brown
Skin: rose beige, pink beige, grey beige, and can be sallow
Eyes: grey brown, rose brown

■ Cool-Light

When light is your second characteristic, you are the softest looking of the cool group. You have a fairer, softer look than the cool-dark, with not so much contrast. You will find the soft blue undertone shades look wonderful on you, but be careful when wearing contrasts, as your look is more subtle and serene. Adding greys or beige to your dark-light contrast combinations, softens the look, making it more unique, and more in tune with your body's neutral look.

■ Cool-Dark

When dark is your second characteristic, your eyes and skin will be medium to deep in intensity. You won't have as much apparent blue or rose undertone to your skin. Your hair won't be quite as ash and you may be able to see some warm. You will have some degree of contrast. The depth of your hair and eyes will generally determine how deep a colour you can wear.

Cool Fans

(From left to right)
Fuchsia
Plum
Blue Red
Grey Navy
Grey Blue
Deep Blue Green
Emerald Green
Lemon Yellow
Rose Beige
Rose Brown

Cool Light

(From left to right)
Soft Burgundy
Soft Fuchsia
Orchid
Powder Pink
Lavender
Powder Blue
Medium Blue Green
Medium Blue Grey
Pastel Blue Green
Light Lemon Yellow

Cool Dark

(From left to right)
Shocking Pink
Magenta
True Red
Royal Purple
Bright Burgundy
Royal Blue
Charcoal Grey
True Green
Bright Yellow
Light True Grey

Neutrals for all cool tonal groups

(From left to right) *White, Soft White, Grey Beige, Cocoa, Light Blue Grey, Medium True Grey, Charcoal Blue Grey, Navy Blue*

SIX GIRLS WEARING THEIR RIGHT COLOURS

Bright-Dark wearing Royal Purple

Muted wearing Olive Green

Dark-Bright wearing True Red

Light-Bright wearing Ivory White

Warm-Dark wearing Peach

Cool-Light wearing Grey Blue

Combining and Wearing all Colours

In this section I want to show you how to start making colour work for you. By now you will have recognised your main tonal group colours and secondary colours, and this (after a little practice) will enable you to recognise colours in your wardrobe which are *not* so good for you. However, with a little ingenuity you can *still* wear the not-so-good colours. Something can always be done with an additional colour to make the not-so-good look better on you. That's why I have included fairly detailed information on the most common neutrals, and how *all* types can adjust and wear them. If you follow this approach you will learn how to manage your wardrobe successfully.

◼ Experimenting with Colour

As an initial exercise, you could go into a fabric department (or use your own wardrobe if it has enough variety of colours). Try to find colours which have the same tonal quality: when you put them together, see how harmonious they are. Or place a bright handkerchief or piece of fabric next to pale or greyed-down colour and see how the bright fabric accentuates their contribution. Next, put some black on to a bright fabric and see how this emphasises it. Alternatively, look at how greys and beiges soften bright colours, and how adding white to brights both brightens and lightens them at the same time. Soft white will always achieve a more sophisticated look no matter how it is used. If you combine it with earthy neutrals, for instance, it will appear sharper and brighter. As you become more adventurous and start to explore further colour innovations, you will begin to understand your own sense of colour, and your eye will develop a certain sophistication. You will suddenly start to see colour in a

new, more exciting way, and will realise the limitless possibilities of colour combinations. Experiment and enjoy it.

◼ Reviewing your Wardrobe

Take the perennially popular colour black, for instance. Many people think they can't wear it, but I am convinced that *everyone* can – the secret is in the way that they wear it, and the colours they wear it with. To utilise colours which are not your best, and to make them look good – inspired, even – you must return to the colour wheels, and look for the colours which will *lift* that black and make it right for you. Don't ever despair if you have a solid black dress or suit hanging in your wardrobe which you never feel happy wearing – you have several options. A black dress could be combined with jewellery, a bolero, jacket or coat in your best colours for a stunning transformation. A suit could have a blouse, jewellery, tie, or hanky in your best colours. Alternatively, the jacket of a suit could be cut down into a bolero to wear with the skirt, so that more of the blouse, in your *best* colours would be showing.

Everyone can wear black on the bottom half of the body anyway; all you have to do is bring just a little colour into the top half to tune with it. With a little imagination, you will be able to find some way to wear it, and even if it isn't quite perfect you still haven't had to throw it away.

◼ Colour Balance

What about the other colours in your wardrobe which you know are not amongst your best? Determine first, with the aid of the wheels, the colours used in its making. For example, if the colour of the item which isn't quite right is grey green, it has been made from blue and yellow with grey added, and by looking on your main characteristic wheel, you can see that you can wear your green with it. Your other options of course, would be your best blue or yellow, and in choosing between them, select the one which says the most about your dominant characteristic, and which suits you the best. This way, you are combining *related* colours.

You could also wear the complementary colour – the one which is on the opposite side of the colour wheel – so you could wear your best red with a grey green. However, when combining complementary colours, you should never wear the same quantity of each colour together as this would not look right. Let's say the grey green item is a mid-calf length dress; you couldn't then just put a hip length red sweater over it, as the proportions of the complementary colour would be all wrong – it would then become dominant. One colour should *complement* the other. You could get the balance right by wearing the grey green dress with a red scarf, brooch or other piece of jewellery, or a grey green suit with a red blouse, or cardigan. The highest percentage ratio of complementary colours should be 40% to 60% main colour (in this case a maximum of 40% red to 60% grey green). A red hip length sweater would have increased the ratio to 50/50 and would unbalance the effect.

As you can see, the art of learning how to use the right proportions of complementary colours is vital. Accent or accessory colours always attract attention, and in this case the accent is red, a bright and strong colour anyway. You would appear unbalanced if you had red earrings, a red scarf, a red belt *and* red shoes, as the eye of the beholder would not know where to look, with such a strident colour everywhere. Remember, *never* over-do the accent colour.

As we have learned, your face is the focal point of your body, and if you have a suit or skirt in one of your not-so-good colours it is very important that you wear one of the colours which emphasise your dominant characteristic near to your face. Choose one of your best neutrals or colours – in a blouse,

top, scarf or necklace – which will tone with your skin, at the same time as having a relationship with the not-so-good colour. Alternatively, you should choose a colour from the same family in your main colour characteristic which will tone with it. You may, however, need to add a third accent to create contrast or to soften, and that will depend on the amount of contrast your body colouring has.

Feel free to experiment and enjoy the wonderful combinations of colours you are now capable of creating and coming up with. Be inventive – the enjoyment of colours is all about finding your own unique style!

Next, I want to turn to the most common neutrals you have hanging in your wardrobe, and show how they can be made to work even better for you now.

Look at the photographs that follow to see how we have added scarves and blouses in the models' *right* colours to complement their not-so-good neutrals and bring their look to life.

Opposite page: *Susie, a Muted, looks sallow in the charcoal sweater and skirt. Adding a flamboyant scarf in muted tones with a bright gold brooch brings her look to life.* (Turn to page 50 for hints on how to wear charcoal).

WEARING BLACK

Every season, fashion colours come and go yet black consistently remains the most popular and useful colour. Once upon a time, almost every woman had the ever-popular 'little black dress' in her wardrobe that she could always fall back on if in doubt about what to wear. Then, with the arrival of the colour and image consultant, thousands, perhaps millions, of women were told never, never to wear black because it's not your colour, it's ageing, it's this, it's that. Throw it out, they were told, and thousands did, never to don black again, but it left a gap in their wardrobes which very few knew how to fill.

Let me just state here, once and for all, that *everyone* can wear black! Here are some ways to wear it, make a fashion statement, and feel good, confident in the knowledge that you've got it right.

▓ Dark Tonal Group

Black, of course, is one of your best neutrals, but should be made to look individual and unique for you. Some darks look stunning and dramatic when dressed all in black, others just need gold or silver jewellery to lift it, but most look better when bringing in their second colour characteristic. For a *Dark-Bright*, the effect black has on bright colours is very striking and dramatic: red gets redder, blue becomes stronger and so on. Those who have a great deal of contrast can also introduce the bright pastels. For a *Dark-Muted*, combining black with a deeper colour intensifies depth and richness. Depending on how warm and muted you can go, will decide what colours you put with your black, but tans, rusts, warm beiges etc. all bring a rich, sophisticated look.

▓ Light Tonal Group

Black is not your best neutral as it can completely take you over if worn solo (see the illustration opposite). Worn on the bottom half of the body in a skirt or trousers, black creates no problem as long as a little is brought up to the top half of the body, with a scarf, brooch etc. But a black dress would only work if it had a low-cut neckline which allowed your skin and a necklace to act as a colour break between your face, eyes and hair, or a jacket, shawl or bolero in one of your best colours or neutrals (see opposite). A *Light-Bright* could add light to medium neutrals to the bright and black combination, and a *Light-Muted* would have to avoid combining black with very light colours as this can give a very sharp aggressive look which does not correspond with the body's signals. Whilst some teenagers like this look, it is much more harmonious if a light to medium neutral is added.

▓ Muted Tonal Group

Great care is needed when combining black with muted tones, as these combinations can appear drab and uninteresting and in most cases a three-colour combination works best. For both *Muted-Darks*, and *Muted-Lights*, adding black to your best neutral and colour combinations can give a fashion statement as opposed to wearing it as your main neutral. You must however experiment; good understanding of your natural colouring is what helps you to succeed and achieve that individual look.

▓ Bright Tonal Group

Brights can, in most cases, add black to their colour combinations; some can even wear black as a main neutral on its own with bright jewellery. Many brights look stunning in black, particularly when it is used to create a sharp contrast as in black-white, but even this look can be enhanced with the addition of a bright hanky, jewellery or scarf. For a dramatic up-beat look, *Bright-Darks* can add black to all the bright clear colours in their tonal group. Some brights wear black better than others, but all brights look best in colour first, and black second or third. *Bright-Lights* can combine black with all the bright colours in their tonal group, but should add light neutrals or colours *before* black for their best look.

■ Warm Tonal Group

Black is not one of your best neutrals but, provided that you wear it in combination with your best neutrals and colours on the top half of the body, or bring in a scarf or jewellery to create a colour break between your face and say, a black dress, you can create a stunning and unique effect. *Warm-Lights* can use warm beige, ivory and warm greys to pull together black and your warm-light group colour. All the medium warm neutral colours of the *Warm-Dark* palette will work well with black, but adding a third colour will unite the colours and make the whole look richer and more interesting.

Below: *Julia, a Light-Bright, is overwhelmed by the plain black dress which is not her best neutral. A scarf in her best light shades instantly corrects the balance.*

■ Cool Tonal Group

When black is used as the main neutral, a sharp image is created by just adding a colour from your main band, and whilst some cools who already have a sharp image can use black successfully in this way, other cools with less sharpness cannot. They should strive to use black as an *addition* to their main neutral and colour combination, especially near the face, or use the skin – as in low necks – or jewellery and scarves as a colour break to the face. All the *Cool-Light* colours will work well with black, but a light to medium neutral might have to be added to some combinations to make them more interesting and less aggressive. *Cool-Darks* can wear all the medium colours of the cool band with black, but light to medium neutrals may be needed to bring it all together, depending where you are on the tonal fan.

WEARING WHITE

White, like black, is always extremely popular. It mixes easily with all colours as well as neutrals, and can be worn by everyone from the waist down and in a pattern combination. White makes light and bright colours seem brighter, while mixing it with the dark toned-down colours can give a very unusual effect. There are many shades of white, and because pure white is a bright neutral and can be found in the tonal bands where 'bright' is, off whites and ivory whites are the ones most people can wear best. But, like all neutrals, it usually needs other colours or neutrals with it to look its best.

Dark Tonal Group

Pure white mixes well with this tonal band and gives it a crisp look. It can be worn all year round and brings life to pattern combinations. Worn alone, it can be too overpowering. For a *Dark-Bright*, adding white both brightens and lightens your colour scheme. It mixes well with all your neutrals, and a dash of colour from the bright colours in your tonal group can be added. Softer warm white to oyster white are the best for *Dark-Warms* to mix with their dark neutrals. A dash of colour can be added.

Light Tonal Group

Adding white to light colours both heightens and lightens them. *Light-Brights* can't go wrong by mixing white with any bright, as any combination has a dazzling effect. If it is too dazzling overall, they can use soft white, or a second neutral, to bring it in line with the body's look. Soft white is the most appropriate white for a *Light-Muted*. It looks white when mixed with light to medium neutrals and softer pastels.

Muted Tonal Group

Your best white is soft white to oyster, and gives a soft sophisticated look when you combine it with your light neutrals. *Muted-Darks* may have to add a beige, or light grey as a buffer between darker colours or neutrals and white.

Bright Tonal Group

White and bright pastels (almost white) are considered brights as they are bright as well as light. *Bright-Darks* can use white as an accent as they can take extreme contrast such as black/white, navy/white etc. For *Bright-Lights*, white with bright pastels gives a dazzling result, which may prove to be *too* light as bright-lights need more colour contrast. Soft white will produce a softer image and goes with all your tonal band colours and neutrals. If you add it to a neutral or light colour, you may require a bright colour.

Warm Tonal Group

Whilst all tonal bands can wear pure white in combination, soft white, ivory and oyster are generally considered the best whites for the warm tonal group. Both *Warm-Lights* and *Warm-Darks* should wear whites with their best colours.

Cool Tonal Group

Pure white mixes well with all the neutrals and colours of the cool tonal group. For a *Cool-Light*, white has a cooling effect on all the light pastel colours, even the ones with a slightly warm undertone. If you find pure white is too bright used solo, use soft white. *Cool-Darks* generally look their best with two added colours or neutrals with white.

Opposite page: *Vanessa, a Dark, loses all her natural vibrancy when she wears an all-white look. Oyster white is her best white. However, the addition of a jewel-coloured jacket and matching brooch and earrings brings her pure white outfit to life.*

WEARING BEIGE

Beige is a good stand-by to fall back on. Choosing the right beige can be tricky, however, so let your skin tone be your guide. If you have visible pink in your skin, as in pink beige or rose brown, you should avoid wearing golden beige near to your face unless you can utilise a colour break, but wearing a non-matching beige away from the skin is not a problem. The reverse is also true: a person with a golden tone to their skin should not wear pink beiges near their face without a break of colour.

■ Dark Tonal Group

Beiges work wonderfully well with the dark tonal bands to make an impressive statement. Beige mixes really well with all the dark neutrals, but for the *Dark-Brights* an additional bright or jewel colour from your tonal group would bring the whole look to life. Beige is really at home with all the rich earthy colours of the *Dark-Muted's* tonal group, but again a third colour works best in combination.

■ Light Tonal Group

Beiges are very useful to the light tonal group as they mix with all the light and darker colours, and so they are excellent used as buffers to bring a lighter and darker colour together. *Light-Brights* can combine beige with the pinks, peaches and aquas of their tonal band. When adding it to the darker colours and neutrals, a third colour or neutral may have to be added. Pink beige is a really good neutral for the *Light-Muted*, as it mixes well with all your pastels, as well as your medium colours and neutrals.

■ Muted Tonal Group

Beiges of all kinds are really excellent neutrals for the muted tonal group, as they combine really well with all neutrals and colours. For *Muted-Darks*, a grey beige is usually best near to the skin, while any beige works well away from the skin. Mix it with all the colours from your tonal band, using it in a three-colour combination. The pink beige is usually the best one to be worn near the *Muted-Light's* skin.

■ Bright Tonal Group

Beige can be a little tricky to mix with brights. A bright outfit with a little beige works well, or bring in a second neutral to lift your colour combinations. If wearing predominantly beige, add a vivid splash of jewel colour (see the photograph opposite). *Bright-Darks* look best in beige with bright colours, but if combining with your dark neutrals, you'll need to add a bright accent for your best look. *Bright-Lights*: a second lighter neutral or a bright pastel may be needed if you're adding a darker neutral in order to keep the look bright and light.

■ Warm Tonal Group

Neutral to warm beiges which make the rich colours look even richer, are the best for this tonal group. *Warm-Lights* should use beige with all their light colours and neutrals and as a buffer between the darker colours and neutrals in a three-colour combination. All the colours and neutrals of the *Warm-Dark's* tonal group work wonderfully well with beiges.

■ Cool Tonal Group

Any neutral beige – without an undertone (warm or cool) – or pink to rose beige mixes well with neutrals and colours of this tonal group. Bearing in mind what has already been said, all the light and dark colours of the *Cool-Light's* tonal group look wonderful with beige. All the slightly calmed-down brights of the *Cool-Dark's* tonal group also go well with beige.

Opposite page: *Susan, a Bright-Dark, looks her best in bright colours, and loses her natural colour in the beige suit and blouse. Her bright look is revealed when she substitutes an emerald green blouse and adds a gold brooch.*

WEARING NAVY

Navy, like black, is a very popular neutral, which is why it is to be found in most people's wardrobes. It is also another dark neutral which needs a light or bright neutral or colour with it to create contrast. Unlike most other dark neutrals, it is worn all year round and it works well with a broad spectrum of colours. Whilst some people don't take the dark navies as well as a lighter or toned-down navy near the face, any navy can be worn in skirts and accessories.

◼ Dark Tonal Group

Navy is one of your best neutrals as it can recreate your body's look with all your light neutrals and brighter colours. It is complimentary to most complexions and works well. For *Dark-Brights*, the primary colours of their tonal group are excellent mixes with navy, as are the jewel colours. Navy and light neutral combinations will need a little bright accessory. All the earthy tones in the *Dark-Muted's* tonal group look particularly effective in combination with navy.

◼ Light Tonal Group

A lighter or slightly greyed-down navy looks best with this tonal group, but any navy can be made to work well, so long as you utilise a break of colour with a blouse, scarf, or jewellery near your face. Use your best neutrals or light colours from your tonal group. For *Light-Brights*, a light clear navy is the best, as it is an excellent mix with all the neutrals, pastels and clear bright colours of the tonal group. For a *Light-Muted*, a greyed-down navy is best, but any navy will mix with the tonal group colours, and these will have a softening effect on the navy.

◼ Muted Tonal Group

A greyed-down or marine navy looks best, but any navy will look good in combination with the neutrals and colours of this tonal group. A marine navy is best for *Muted-Darks*, but any navy will work so long as you add the muted-dark colours of the tonal group and keep the contrast level down. A greyed-down navy is best for *Muted-Lights*, but adding the muted-light colours from your tonal group to any navy will work if a little thought goes into it.

◼ Bright Tonal Group

Bright navy is one of the best neutrals for the bright tonal group, and goes well with all your tonal group colours and neutrals. For a *Bright-Dark*, a clear navy is best, but the tonal group works well with any navy. If a third colour is desired add a light neutral. All the light true colours of the *Bright-Light's* tonal group mix well with navy, but you may need to add your light neutrals. A navy dress or suit with your best white will need a bright accessory.

◼ Warm Tonal Group

Marine navy is your best, but all shades of navy combine well with the earthy tones of your tonal group. (See the photograph opposite.) *Warm-Lights* should add the lighter warm colours of their tonal group, and the medium to dark colours will need a light neutral or colour with them to make the whole look warm and light. All the warm medium colours of the *Warm-Dark's* tonal group go well with navy.

◼ Cool Tonal Group

Whilst grey navy is best, and bright navy can seem to be *too* bright for some cool people, clever blending with your tonal group colours can soften it down. For a *Cool-Light*, soft powder pinks, yellow blue and light blue green all have a softening effect on navy. Stronger colours like watermelon red with navy may need a soft neutral to accompany them. Jewel colours are good for *Cool-Darks*.

Opposite page: *Our model, Wei San, is a Warm-Dark. Although the plain navy dress looks dramatic, it drains her face of its natural colour. Adding a multi-coloured scarf in warm tones makes all the difference.*

WEARING DARK CHOCOLATE BROWN

Dark chocolate brown does not enjoy the same popular appeal as black, charcoal or navy, but remains a very good dark neutral, which looks stunning on the right person, or with the right combination of colours.

Dark Tonal Group

This is considered one of your best dark neutrals. It is less dramatic than black, but can make some interesting, even exotic, mixes! For a *Dark-Bright*, it works well with all the bright tonal groups as it helps bring out the vividness of the colours. It also works well with the neutrals. If mixing it with black, you'll need a third brighter colour. For your best look brown can bring a richness to the *Dark-Muted's* colour combinations, especially with black.

Light Tonal Group

The medium to light browns look best on someone in the light tonal group, but with a little care dark chocolate brown can be made to look good mixed with the light to medium neutrals and colours. All the light-bright colours from the *Light-Bright's* tonal group look good with brown, but you will need a lighter colour or neutral added to the combination to create a light-bright look. All the light dusty tones from the *Light-Muted's* tonal group give a soft effect when mixed with brown. With some soft shades, you will need a light neutral to lift the brown.

Muted Tonal Group

All the *Muted-Dark's* shades of beige enhance dark chocolate brown by their neutrality, and all the slight warm undertone colours blend well. Just add a third light neutral or colour when the combination becomes too dark, or use coffee brown instead. For the *Muted-Light*, the dusty tones go well with brown, and for a three-colour combination think, light/medium/dark chocolate brown.

Bright Tonal Group

Dark chocolate brown, like charcoal, makes an excellent neutral if used in combination with this tonal group. The deep brown shade of a *Bright-Dark's* hair is a wonderful neutral already, but, like all neutrals in your tonal group, a colour needs to be added to bring it in line with your body's colouring. As the colours get darker you will have to add a lighter neutral or a bright pastel (white with a hint of colour), leaving it still bright and clear. For a *Bright-Light*, the best brown is medium. Use medium to light colours and neutrals to make it look lighter and brighter. If they are medium/dark, you need to add a third colour or neutral to give it a lift.

Warm Tonal Group

Although dark chocolate brown has dark as its first characteristic, warm is its second, so it has a tonal relationship with all the warm colours. For *Warm-Lights*, keeping the light colours high up and dark chocolate brown low down, it can be used fully. If the stronger colours appear too vivid, use a third light neutral to tone them down. This is one of the *Warm-Dark's* best neutrals, as it can be blended with anything in the tonal group. You can even mix it with black provided that you add a third neutral or colour to the combination.

Cool Tonal Group

Dark chocolate brown mixes well with cool band colours (see the photograph opposite). *Cool-Lights* should use all the light colours and neutrals of their tonal group and use a three-colour combination when adding medium to dark colours.

All the jewel-like colours of the *Cool-Dark's* tonal group contrast well with dark brown. Bringing in a third colour or neutral can add more dimension and makes for a more interesting combination.

Opposite page: *Lynne, a Cool/Light, is taken over by the 'warm' chocolate brown dress she is wearing. The delicacy of her skin tone and cool blue eyes are brought out by the addition of a pale blue scarf and silver earrings worn as a brooch.*

WEARING CHARCOAL

Charcoal offers the depth, drama and useful qualities of black without the harshness, but it has less impact on its own. It is a very useful neutral and it can be used very successfully when combined with your best colours and neutrals. Soft neutrals and bright colours give it a more conventional look; darker, jewel-like colours make it more sophisticated. Adding it to all other shades of grey to create contrast adds interest.

■ Dark Tonal Group

Charcoal grey is one of your best neutrals – you can combine it with almost anything and it is well suited for formal wear. It is a good neutral for bright colours and darker jewel tones, at the same time combining well with the light neutrals. Add it as an accessory to your lighter or brighter looks and it can add dimension and bring those looks more in line with your body's natural colouring. When a *Dark-Bright* wears a neutral with charcoal grey, adding a touch of colour will bring it more in line. All the neutrals and medium intensity *Dark-Muted* colours look good with charcoal.

■ Light Tonal Group

Charcoal is your best 'black'. It combines well with the light neutrals and soft pastels of your tonal group, although the contrast may be too harsh for the *Light-Muted*. If so, you will need a medium neutral added to soften the charcoal and unite it with your tonal colours – for instance, charcoal/medium grey/soft white. Charcoal tones well with all light and bright colours for the *Light-Bright*, but *both* aspects should be added.

■ Muted Tonal Group

Most of the colours in your tonal group have a tonal relationship with charcoal grey, as grey has been used in their making. It will look too dark on most muted types if it is used on its own, but can look wonderful if used in combination with other neutrals and colours from your tonal group near your face. (See the photograph on page 39.) The medium intensity colours of the *Muted-Dark* mix well with charcoal, and a three-colour combination would bring individuality. *Muted-Lights* should use a medium neutral or colour as a go-between with charcoal.

■ Bright Tonal Group

Charcoal is a good neutral for brights as it mixes well with all the bright colours and light neutrals of this group. It also offers a contrasting look which all brights need. It is a good alternative to black where black is too strong and takes over. *Bright-Darks* could also use charcoal, one of their best neutrals, as an accent colour, as can *Bright-Lights*. Wearing charcoal *en masse* may take the *Bright-Lights* over, so they should bring a bright-light look to charcoal, with a third colour.

■ Warm Tonal Group

Charcoal will bring a certain amount of contrast to your look and it mixes comfortably with warm neutrals and your warm colours. It offers a wide range of mixing possibilities. Charcoal not only mixes well with the tones of the *Warm-Light* tonal group, but it can also have a calming-down effect on some of the brights. It offers a sophisticated and interesting image when combined with the *Warm-Dark's* tonal group colours and neutrals.

■ Cool Tonal Group

Charcoal becomes a very useful neutral for the cools who find black creates too sharp an image for them. It combines well with all their tonal colours and light neutrals and makes a good accessory colour. The *Cool-Lights* should use all their light neutrals and light colours. Charcoal is one of the *Cool-Dark's* best neutrals and can be mixed and matched with all their tonal group colours and neutrals.

The Psychology of Colour

Each colour has its own 'feeling' and we, in turn, all have different feelings towards colour. Do you think of red as dangerous and life-threatening (blood and fire), or exciting (fireworks and stimulation)? What about black? Do you find it authoritative and sombre, or sophisticated and sexy?

Research into the psychological effects of colour is still inconclusive, so there is some confusion surrounding why we feel the way we do. There is some evidence to suggest that *how* the light enters the eye – which can be unique to you – can affect the pituitary gland. This gland controls the entire endocrine system, including the thyroid and sex glands, and also the moods associated with them. This could explain why we all perceive colour differently.

But in addition to this we have all had experiences in our past which hold a colour association for us. For instance, I would never have a green and white kitchen as it reminds me of the Second World War when everything was painted green, cream, or brown. Some people don't like wearing the colour of their school uniform! One of the best ways, I have found, to help people understand their own emotional and physical responses to colour, and how these influence their thinking in different situations, is to ask them to close their eyes and imagine the following scenes.

You have just won a holiday in Hawaii and you are day-dreaming a little. What colours are you thinking in? Sunny yellows, bright reds, warm blues? What are all the people wearing in your day-dream? Do the colours you are thinking in make you feel carefree and happy? Think of Cliff Richard singing 'We're all going on a summer holiday'. Has that lifted your spirits even higher? (An experiment on sound and colour together showed that sound enhanced the sensation of colour in the mind.)

Now for a change of scene, think back to the last funeral you attended. What springs to mind – is it dark and sombre colours, depressing music and feelings?

▥ Applying Colour Psychology

Just as colours are associated with past experiences and different sorts of moods or emotions, so they can affect the state of mind of both wearer and onlooker. You can use colour in your clothes to alter how people 'see' you and 'feel' about you.

To look more dynamic at work, and to help you feel more in charge and authoritative, you should wear the darkest neutrals of your main colour characteristic. Use your basic colours for accents and your light neutrals to create contrast. This look is ideal if you are in business, a 'corporate woman', as it not only ensures you look good, but it helps you feel the part by increasing your confidence. It is also useful for other professions to know this, so they understand how to adapt their colours for dress when dealing with the corporate world.

If your work demands a more friendly approach, as in the communications world or 'people business', you should wear your medium neutrals, and accent with your basic colours and light neutrals for a softer look. Wearing these less harsh colour combinations will help you feel more relaxed, and you'll look more friendly and approachable. In turn people will approach *you* more, and will extend a more friendly openness towards you.

The brighter colours in your tonal group are attention-grabbing. These colours are exciting, and they are ideal for wearing to give talks and presentations to large audiences, whether in a large hall or on camera. They will help you to hold people's attention and will give you a firm but friendly, approachable look. Wearing light neutrals to give a presentation in a large hall would make you fade into the background, and your darker neutrals would look too dark; adding something bright to both these would help solve the problem.

If you want to change your mood to fit into a more high-spirited one, and add a little 'pizzazz' to your life, wear your bright colours. Mixing bright colours together creates action – you'll feel much more like running or getting involved in some other energetic activity when you are dressed in and surrounded by bright combinations of colours. Consider for a moment what a disco would be like without the bright flashing lights – another instance where colour also heightens the 'action'.

Adding your light to your bright colours, you will get a more carefree, light-hearted feeling – rather like when nature changes from its dark foliage of winter to the light colours of spring. Don't you feel light-hearted in these colours? Do you get a spring in your step?

Then there are times when you want to create a mood of peace and tranquillity, when you really do not want to be noticed, when you want to fade into the background, to switch off from the high pressure of the day. Wearing your softer neutrals with the lighter colours of your tonal group will help you and the people around you to relax, as colour can have the same calming effect on the beholder. A fashion buyer friend, for instance, lives in grey after her hectic week. I, too, tend to change into the softer shades of my tonal group in the evening to calm me down – far more effective than a drink for winding down!

■ The Colour Test

Let's test your psychological reactions to colour now. First tick the boxes opposite for a quick reaction response.

For an insight into your own colours, turn back to pages 24–35, the tonal groups of your first and second characteristic, and look at each colour individually. Close your eyes, and 'feel' the picture or mood it conveys. Pencil a (1) at the side of all the colours that convey authority or assertiveness. Pencil a (2) at the side of all the colours that make you feel more friendly or approachable. Pencil a (3) at the side of all the colours that lift your spirits and make you feel happy. Pencil a (4) at the side of all the colours which are soothing and calming to you. Pencil a (5) at the side of all the colours which make you feel aggressive – and so on if you have further colour reactions.

This is only a rough guide, of course, but it can help you decide more swiftly what colours to wear when you're going to an important meeting where you have to have an authoritative look, for instance, or to a party where you would like to get into the carefree spirit of things. Keep a note of your number-coded reactions to these colours, and keep it together with your organiser (see page 127) as a handy reference guide so you will avoid buying clothes in the wrong colour on impulse.

Colours can and do dictate your mood, rather like setting the stage of a play for the next big scene in a theatre. But by choosing colours whose 'psychology' you understand in relation to *yourself*, you have made sure you feel *right*. A shy, retiring girl, for instance, would almost certainly not welcome the response that wearing a bright red dress to a party would bring – she wouldn't want to draw attention to herself. Similarly, a very vivacious, outgoing girl would probably not feel at ease dressed from head to toe in drab brown, as her character would demand that she is noticed.

This test is devised to fix in your mind how you feel about the colours. To go into *deep* psychological explanations as to why you might be positive about one colour and negative about another is beyond the scope of this book – and probably of my expertise, despite my having worked with colour for so long! Suffice to say that if you react negatively to a colour, then you shouldn't really wear it, as you won't ever feel entirely happy in it.

EMOTIONAL RESPONSE TO COLOUR

Do you see,

RED as exciting ☐   or dangerous ☐

BLUE as calming ☐   or cold ☐

GREEN as envious, superstitious ☐   or uplifting, rebirth (as of spring) ☐

YELLOW as cheerful ☐   or nauseating ☐

ORANGE as outgoing and warm ☐   or overpowering ☐

PURPLE as confusing ☐   or regal ☐

BLACK as sophisticated ☐   or drab ☐

COLOUR PSYCHOLOGY AT HOME

To get a true idea of the effect that colour has on our mood, I want to turn now to the most obvious example, the use of colour in our surroundings. I actually discovered the dramatic effects of colour on the mind and our moods very early on in my career, when I began mixing paints for my family's decorating business, and realised that use of colour could alter perspectives as well.

There are many factors to consider when choosing colours for your home, but analysing who is going to use the room – and therefore the best *mood* to create in that room – should be the main one. The last chapter will have helped you to understand your own emotional response to colour, and you can now use your new-found knowledge to test other members of your household. For instance, those who work in a dull environment may like a bright room in which to recharge their batteries; whilst others in high-pressure work may require a tranquil, peaceful environment to come home to.

I give below a brief outline of the effects of colour in our surroundings. This illustrates how we all perceive colour differently and therefore all react differently to it.

THE EFFECTS OF COLOUR

THE MOOD YOU WANT TO CREATE	HOW TO ACHIEVE IT	THE COLOURS TO USE	DIFFERENT KINDS OF REACTIONS
DRAMATIC SOPHISTICATED AUSTERE STERILE	Use sharp contrast (not easy to relax in)	Black and white, deep green and deep red or any dark colour with a strong contrast	Smart and stunning, or cold and calculating
HARMONIOUS TRANQUIL RELAXING	Use very little contrast (restful)	Grey and camel, pale blue, pale green and lilac or any harmonious colours which do not have a big contrast	Gentle and calming; or dull and uninteresting
FRIENDLY WELCOMING	Use very warm undertones, of medium intensity (homely)	Browns and beiges and pale pink or soft red or any colours which have a warm friendly feel about them	Inviting and cosy; or smothering and claustrophobic
SUNNY HIGH-SPIRITED	Use bright and light colours (holiday bright feeling)	Yellow and white or any colours which make you feel light-hearted	Cheerful, giving a lift; or loud and cheap

◼ Decorating Rooms

Before redecorating a room, you should look at the fixed colours (the ones you can't change, if any) which have to be lived with, like a fitted carpet or bathroom suite. Using all the information you have learned about colour – the use of complementary and related colours, how you can add one colour to another to either heighten, intensify, or soften and make more subdued – will enable you to deal with fixed colours, even making them look fresh and new.

Colours can also define space and temperature. To see colour affecting space, hold this page at arm's length, and examine both the black and the white balls. Which is closer to you, the black or the white? Which is bigger, the black or white? The black should be closer and the white bigger. Close your eyes and imagine you are picking the balls up. Which do you imagine is the heaviest? It's probably the black. Actually, it's all an illusion, as both balls are really the same size and weight.

SPATIAL TEST

To take this idea further, go back to the six main tonal wheels on page 20. You will clearly see how the dark tonal wheel looks closer than the light one, the warm looks closer than the cool, and the bright looks closer than the muted. By understanding these principles you will see how easy it is to use colour to change the shape of a room by making a high ceiling look lower, a low ceiling look higher, a small room look longer and vice versa, and a long narrow room look more square.

The use of colour to change temperature is probably more familiar. For a warm sunny feel to a room, add some colour from the warm tonal wheel. A clever use of colour could almost help to keep down central heating bills!

Some final snippets on colour in homes, shops and offices. It has been noted that many people's blood pressure goes up when in a room that's all red; they can also become irritated and irritable. Colour psychology has also been used by one international fast-food chain: the bright colours used on the outside of the restaurants are bright and attractive (irresistible to children), while the colours inside are a combination of brights designed to make you eat up and leave fast!

The most important thing for you to recognise and understand in the wonderful world of colour is how to use colour to create a desired effect, to know what colours go well together and why, which harmonise and contrast, and with this will come the confidence to colour yourself and your home with style.

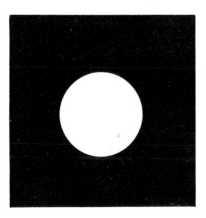

PART TWO

FIGURE IMAGE
CONFIDENCE

Looking objectively at yourself (instead of longingly at a friend or film star), and learning how to emphasise your body's good points and how to camouflage the not-so-good, doesn't just happen on its own. It all needs total honesty, conscious effort, practice and know-how. If you try to deceive yourself about your body shape you will never look your best. So spend time on it *now* and you will then avoid those wasted hours of frustration, and 'fighting' with an unruly wardrobe. You will gain tremendous confidence from the knowledge that you are always looking just right.

Broadly speaking, we all fall into one of six body shapes – curved, heart, ellipse, pear, straight and angular. Clothes which echo your body line will flatter it and look natural on you. For example, if you are straight up and down, you probably feel a little uncomfortable in curvy blouses and dresses with a soft line, whereas a suit with a straight skirt and plain jacket with straight lines makes you feel right.

When you are aware of your body shape you will realise why there are some clothes in your wardrobe which you very rarely wear. The cut of the garment simply does not suit the shape of your body. You can use camouflage (shoulder pads, etc) to draw attention away from bad points or proportional imbalances, but your shape should be your guide in selecting your best styles.

You must have noticed curvaceous ladies looking lumpy and unattractive when squeezed into very fitted suits with straight lines. Yet when you see them in clothes with softer, curved lines such as a gently draped neckline, and a light fabric flowing skirt you will will instantly see the difference.

Conversely, you will probably have seen very bony, angular girls looking all wrong in low-cut, hip-hugging dresses designed for a curvier body. Put them in sharp, geometric lines which balance up their wide shoulders and slim hips, and they look sensational.

As you can see, once you understand the principles of figure image and clothing style, you will avoid buying those clothes which don't seem to suit you as well as you had hoped. Soon your eye will pick out the shapes which look best on you. You will gain the confidence to shop alone, and not rely on the opinions of over-zealous shop assistants, or friends who might be basing their ideas on their *own* figure image.

As well as the six body shapes, there are eight face shapes which also need to be taken into account. They are: round, heart, oval, pear, oblong, square, rectangle and diamond. A round face usually goes with a curved body, and a diamond face with an angular body. Again, it is important that your clothes complement your face shape, and don't fight it or detract from it. After all, your face is what people notice first, and what you want to draw attention to.

Therefore, learning to recognise your own face and body shape is the first and most important move, then you go on to discover if your shoulders, waist and legs are in visual balance. This will lead you to recognise what steps, if any, need to be taken so you can choose the clothes that suit you best and can create a look unique to you, one which you will always feel poised and confident with.

So, let's first see how to discover which body image and face image is *yours*. All you need for a totally honest self-appraisal are these simple props:

1   a full-length mirror (or, better, two)
2   a straight stick or broom handle
3   three pieces of white tape or string, one piece 12 inches (30 cm) long to reveal your face shape, one piece the length of the stick or broom handle, and another to fasten around the waist.
4   two weights (a couple of washers, curtain weights, or empty cotton reels)
5   some drawing pins or tacks

Attach the weight(s) to one end of the string or tape, and attach the other end with pins or tacks to one end of the stick or broom handle. You now have a plumb line which will reveal your body shape to you. Then attach another weight to the end of the 12 inch (30 cm) string or tape and you have a plumb line to reveal your face shape.

If you use these few props correctly you will have no trouble in deciding which of the six body shapes and eight face shapes are yours.

Find Your Face Shape and Direction

Finding your face shape is a very good way of determining which clothing lines you should wear near your face (see page 100), and it also helps you discover your figure image and what helps to make you unique. You will easily identify the basic face shapes by looking at the following illustrations and following the guidelines.

Using the 12 inch (30 cm) plumb line, and looking into the mirror, place the string on the temple bone, that is the bone at the side of your forehead and allow the plumb line to hang down straight and free. Which face shape below best describes you?

ROUND

Your face will curve outwards away from the straight line of the string on your plumb line around the cheek area, giving a definite indication of curve.

HEART

The widest part of the face is at the forehead and you will see a curve inwards away from the straight line of the string from a broad forehead to a narrower jaw line.

OVAL

The forehead is slightly wider than the rest of the face and you will see a gentle tapering inwards from the string to the jaw line.

PEAR

A narrow forehead with straight-angular lines to the face, which will move outside the string to a wide, almost straight jaw line.

OBLONG

The string will generally hang straight from the forehead to the jaw line which will be equal in width and narrow in comparison to the length of the face. Cheeks can curve out slightly from the plumb line and the corners will be gently curved.

SQUARE

The width of the face can be equal or almost equal to the length of it, with forehead, cheeks and jaw being in a straight or almost straight line following the plumb line.

RECTANGLE

Very straight lines to the face, which is narrow in comparison to the length. Forehead, cheeks and jaw are straight, following the plumb line.

DIAMOND

A narrow forehead and chin, and the cheeks have angular lines which extend beyond the plumb line.

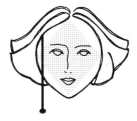

Find Your Figure Image

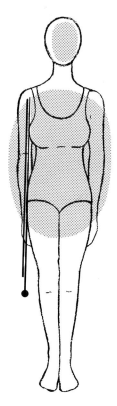

The next step is just as easy. This is how you discover which category your body falls into.

Once again stand in front of the full-length mirror, and, using the pole and plumb line, place the pole down the side of your body, finding and resting the pole on your widest part. Let the top of the pole rest on the edge of your shoulder bone, which is directly above the armpit, allowing the plumb line to hang free. The degree of variation from the straight plumb line to the pole will make your body shape become instantly obvious.

- If the plumb line hangs next to the pole, then you are a straight
- If the plumb line hangs next to the pole but you have a definite waist, then you are a curved
- If the plumb line hangs next to the pole, but your thighs taper strongly inwards, then you are an ellipse
- If, however, the pole goes strongly outwards, then you are a pear shape
- If the pole slopes inwards, you are angular, or heart-shaped (see the drawings to work out which type you are)

Look at the drawings and the descriptions and identify your own figure image. As a rough guideline, oval, heart or round face shapes usually match the curved and heart-shaped body lines; oblong, oval or pear-shaped faces mainly ally themselves with ellipse and pear-shaped body lines; and diamond, square or rectangular face shapes usually go with straight and angular body lines.

1 CURVED/HOURGLASS

You will have softly rounded curves, which are well defined in the body and face. Your shoulders have a softly rounded look, with the curve extending to the top of your arm. Your hip line is generally centrally located between your waist and thighs, giving you a definite waist and slim thighs. Your body will curve inward from the straight of the stick and the plumb line at the waist, and outwards to the stick around the bust and hip area, giving a definite hourglass or figure-of-eight look to your body.

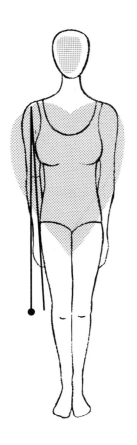

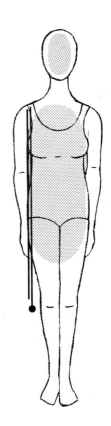

2 HEART

You have broad, rounded shoulders, with your upper arm generally the widest area on your body. You can be large busted, top heavy even, with slimmer looking waist, hips and thighs. The bottom half of you tapers and is visually narrower and can be straighter looking. You have a flat, high hipbone and will look taller than you are, because your heaviness is at the top. The straight of the plumb line will hang away from the bottom half of your body, and the stick will slope inwards from your shoulder.

3 ELLIPSE

You can be oval, giving a gentle curved look, or rectangular with soft tapered edges giving a gentle straight look. The gentle curved look has a slightly rounder and heavier looking body than the gentle straight ellipse, with tapered to sloping shoulders, but both have waists which are broad in comparison to the shoulders, flat hips and thighs, which taper inwards. The body leans towards the stick away from the straight of the plumb line at the waist area, then the body tapers to a slim looking thigh.

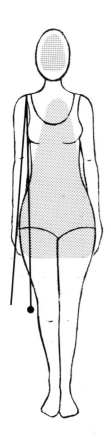

4 PEAR

You have slim shoulders and broad hips giving a pear shape to the body. The amount of curve or straightness you see between the pole and the plumb line will be the best guide to follow for your clothing line. Usually it will depend on how much weight you are carrying. You will have a tendency to look shorter than you are, because of the wide bone structure at the thigh area. Your body will go away from the plumb line towards the pole, starting around the hip area down to the thigh and upper leg area.

5 STRAIGHT

You can be slightly angular or square, and you're not necessarily thin. There are no obvious curves, and you have square shoulders, and a flat high hip. You can have a slightly tapered hip, which is a slope outwards from hip to thigh, but *thigh* bone would be straight with shoulder bone. The plumb line and stick will be in line right down the body.

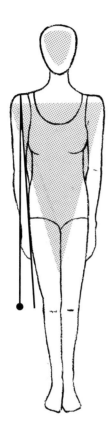

6 ANGULAR

You have broad shoulders in comparison with your straight, narrow hips and thighs, and flat, high hipbones. You can be quite thin, and your body is angular without curves. The plumb line will hang away from the body, and the stick will slant inwards from the shoulder towards the body.

Your Figure Image

Once you have done the plumb line test, circle the number of the figure image which best describes you:

1 Curved/Hourglass

2 Heart

3 Ellipse

4 Pear

5 Straight

6 Angular

Remember this number as it will be significant in the next part of the book, the one relating to style confidence.

Visual Body Balance

Once you have discovered your face shape and your figure image, you need to consider how visually balanced your body is. Height is relevant too, but this is usually obvious: if you are 5' 3" and under you are small; 5' 4"/5' 5", you are considered medium; and if you are 5' 6" and over you are tall.

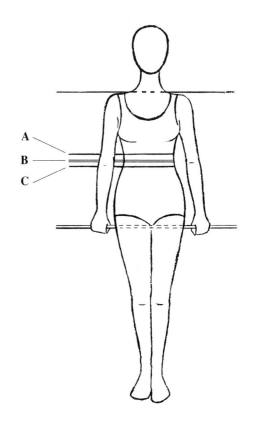

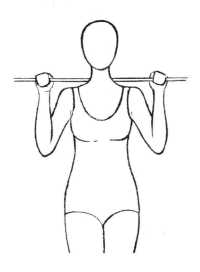

SHOULDERS

Taking your pole, place it at the back of your neck across your shoulders. Pull down on the pole evenly to make sure it is level with the base of the neck, and see how much drop there is from the stick and the outer edge of your shoulder. If it's less than 1 inch (2.5 cm), your shoulders are very straight; less than 1½ inches (4 cm), straight; about 2 inches (5 cm), the shoulders are tapered; more than 2 inches (5 cm), your shoulders are sloping.

WAIST

Now tie a piece of string or tape around your waist. Take your pole, hold it with both hands across your lower bottom, and slightly sit on it. Now compare the space between the shoulders and the string and the string and the pole. The string should be equally balanced between your shoulders and your bottom. If it is, no adjustment is needed. If, however, your top half is longer than your bottom half, you are long waisted; if vice versa, you're short waisted. Both these have to be taken into consideration.

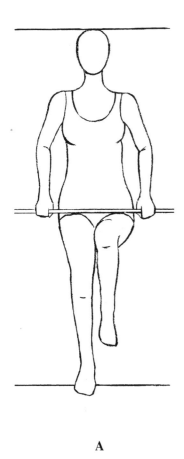

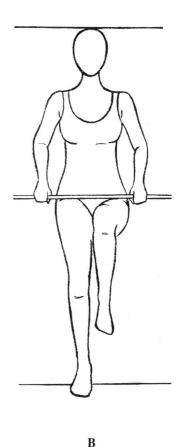

A

B

LEGS

To discover if your legs are short or long – usually fairly obvious! – place the pole horizontally across the leg-hip crease. Lift one of your legs to hold the pole in the crease. Now compare the body lengths above and below the leg-line stick. Are your legs below the pole balanced or longer than the rest of your body? If yes, there's no problem. If your legs are shorter than your body length, you'll have to take this into consideration on the chart on page 73.

Key to page 64 (right)

A = *short waist*
B = *balanced waist*
C = *long waist*

Key to page 65

A = *short legs*
B = *long legs*

Accentuate the Positive

One crucial thing to remember is never give up on yourself. We *all* have good and positive points about our bodies, regardless of height and weight, so we should draw people's attention to these, and away from the negative and not-so-good points. I have divided possible positive points into four columns, and you should ring the one from each that you consider *your* best.

Column A relates to how you can emphasise your best points by a clever use of colour – for instance by making the most of auburn hair, clear skin, green eyes or full red lips. You will achieve the best look for yourself by wearing make-up shades which tone and harmonise with your colour fan. Turn to pages 24–26 for how to accentuate *these* positive points.

After reading this book and learning about colour in general and about your own colouring you will recognise what suits you best. Your face is always the focal point, so use colours in clothes, accents *and* makeup which will draw attention to it.

Columns B, C and D are *figure* columns, and by circling your best feature in each column, and remembering the 'code' – B (bust) or C (thighs) – you will be able to relate these best points to the style notations or numbers on pages 78–93.

You'll learn more about making the most of your figure in the next few pages, and in *Part Three, Style Confidence*, but first, here are a few simple suggestions. If you have a good neck, do as I suggest on page 96, and draw attention to it: wear a jewel there, or a neckline that really flatters your face and figure image.

If you have a good waist, wear waisted lines, or pin some brooches or wear decorative belts there (see pages 83/5 and 92/3). If you have good thighs, wear lines that draw attention to them – tapered clothes or clothes that end, in line or colour, on or near the thighs, such as short skirts, or jackets and cardigans that end at this area and will therefore draw attention to it.

A	B	C	D
hair	neck	hips	arms
skin	shoulders	stomach	legs
eyes	bust	bottom	calves
lips	waist	thighs	ankles

Eliminate the Negative

A figure negative has to be a *real* problem, a definite figure imbalance which can be easily seen by others, before it can be called a problem. For example, if your shoulders are narrower than your hips or thighs (pear shape), and you are not using any methods of camouflage, it is quite obvious to others that your hips or thighs are out of balance and are wider than the rest of your body. (This particular imbalance can be easily corrected, for instance, just by wearing shoulder pads which should make each shoulder 1–1½ inches/2.5–4 cm wider than the widest part of your body.)

When you come to assess figure negatives you will have to determine whether your problems are real or a figment of your imagination; they may just be a slight problem which doesn't really need to be corrected, or one which disappears completely with some minor camouflage like the shoulder pads. The main thing to ask yourself is, is it obvious to others?

Let us begin by looking at the following pictures and descriptions. Circle the number or the B on each line which best describes you. The B stands for *balanced* – which means you have no problems! The numbers stand for figure faults and relate directly to style, which we look at in the next section on style confidence.

Short neck, double chin

Extra long neck

Balanced

7   B   8

Wear open or low necklines, or an eye-catching necklace ending half-way between neck and bust to create the illusion of length. Avoid chokers and chunky necklaces which cut your body line up.

Wear your low-necked tops and dresses with a blouse, scarf, or short necklace which does not extend below the collar bone, or buy some add-on collars like turtle, mandarin etc.

Narrow, sloping shoulders

Balanced

Extra broad shoulders

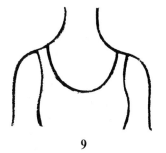

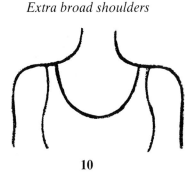

9　　　　　　**B**　　　　　　**10**

Shoulder pads will give an immediate result, making the shoulders 1–1½ inches (2.5–5 cm) wider than your widest part. They make your body more visually balanced.

If they're broader than the rest of your body, then remove shoulder pads. Wear collars which point anywhere but at your shoulders. Wear eye-catching earrings, necklaces and lapel clips which bring the eye away from the shoulders.

Heavy arms

Balanced

Thin arms

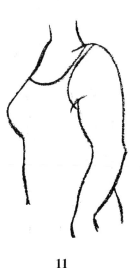

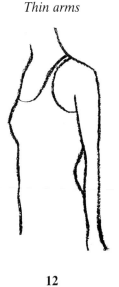

11　　　　　　**B**　　　　　　**12**

Wear shoulder pads designed to continue the shoulders over the thickest part of the arm, allowing the sleeve hang to the hand to be unrestricted.

Drape scarves or stoles around your shoulders, or wear long sleeves, slim bracelets or delicate chain links.

Large low bust

Balanced

Little or no bust

13   B   **14**

Wear a good, well-fitting bra which lifts and separates. At the same time create shoulder interest or highlight other parts of your body. Avoid detail on the bustline.

Emphasise your shoulders, or your waist, and wear a jacket with interesting lapels or add jewellery to them. Gathered yokes, bust details like pockets, or a low-scalloped bodice, all add interest.

Short waist

Balanced

Long waist

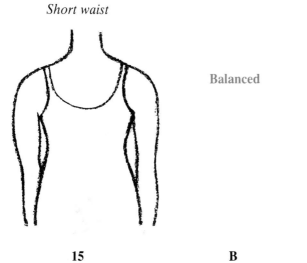

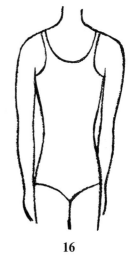

15   B   **16**

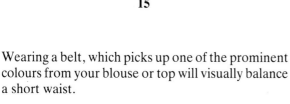

Wearing a belt, which picks up one of the prominent colours from your blouse or top will visually balance a short waist.

Wearing a belt which picks up the prominent colour of your skirt will visually heighten your waist.

Thick waist

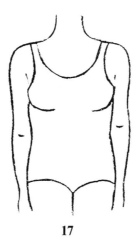

17

Wear shoulder pads so that your shoulders are at least 1 inch (2.5 cm) wider. This makes your shoulders look broader and your waist slimmer. If your problem is excessive only wear belts when wearing a jacket or cardigan open. Wear accessories which attract the eye to a more positive part of your body.

Slightly prominent stomach

Very prominent stomach

Balanced

B

B

18

Avoid waisted designs, or wear loose unstructured jackets or long cardigans over your dresses and skirts. If wearing a belt, make it very loose, with only the middle centre or buckle visible.

Very prominent bottom

19

As with very prominent stomach.

Balanced

Flat bottom

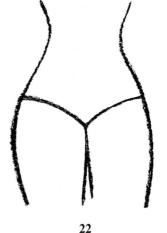

B

20

Take attention away from the area by using bold line design and colour.

Wide hips

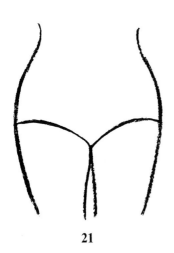

21

Avoid anything ending at the hip area; end tops higher or lower. Wear your belts slack as pulling them in to make your waist look smaller ensures that your hips look bigger.

Balanced

Large thighs

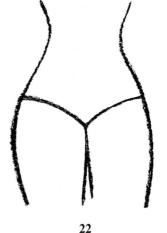

B

22

Wear eye-catching accessories near the face to take the eye away from your thighs. Use shoulder pads to balance your look.

Short legs   Balanced   Long legs

23   **B**   **B**

Streamline your legs by wearing shoes, tights and hemlines in the same colour. Balance your hemline to show enough leg to give visual balance.

Thin legs   Broad calves, thick ankles

Balanced

24   **B**   **25**

Wide bulky skirts make your legs look thinner, so slimmer skirts are best. Avoid hemline detail, fancy shoes, and contrasts. Wear patterned tights when appropriate.

Avoid fancy shoes, contrast colours, and hemline detail – these will only emphasise your worst point.

The Key to Your Own Personal Image

3 best points	3 worst points

B ....

C ....

D ....

Figure image

1	Curved/hourglass	4	Pear
2	Heart	5	Straight
3	Ellipse	6	Angular

Figure negatives

7	Short neck, double chin	17	Thick waist
8	Extra long neck	18	Very prominent stomach
9	Narrow and sloping shoulders	19	Very prominent bottom
10	Broad shoulders	20	Flat bottom
11	Heavy arms	21	Wide hips
12	Thin arms	22	Large thighs
13	Large or low bust	23	Short legs
14	Little or no bust	24	Thin legs, thin ankles
15	Short waist	25	Broad calves, thick ankles
16	Long waist		

■ Fill in the B, C, D – your three best figure points – from page 66. These you need to *emphasise*. Pencil these in, too, on the central boxes on the style pages in the next section.

■ Next, look at the numbers 1 to 6, your figure image, and tick off the one you are closest to. Pencil this number in on the left-hand box on the style pages following.

■ Numbers 7 through to 25 refer to the body area which you consider a problem and which needs to be camouflaged. Look at them carefully and ring those that you consider to be a problem. Fill in your three

worst points. Write the numbers of your three worst points in the boxes on the right-hand side of the style pages following.

■ For example, if you are medium height, pear-shaped, with large hips, a small bust, a flat stomach, a slim waist and arms and thick calves, *your* boxes on the following style pages would look like this:

Figure type

4

Best points

waist	stomach	arms

Worst points

21	25	14

PART THREE

STYLE CONFIDENCE

Now that the most difficult part is over – making a thorough and honest examination of yourself – you will be familiar with your face shape, body image, your good points and your not-so-good points so you can now begin to discover the best style lines to wear.

At the top of the following pages there are boxes in which you will have pencilled (or *will* pencil!) your figure numbers as a constant reminder. Also in the following pages we have drawn various types of neckline, jacket, skirt, trouser and sleeve shapes etc., all of which emphasise some parts of the body and camouflage others. To balance the body visually and to make sure you pick the right styles for you, we have given each article of clothing various numbers – the numbers of the figure positives or negatives in the last section.

The styles which indicate a tick ($\sqrt{}$) at the side of the numbers on your list are not only good styles for you, but they will also help to camouflage and take attention away from your particular figure imbalance. The styles which indicate a cross ($\times$) at the side of the numbers on your list will draw attention to your figure problem and you should only wear them when adequate thought has been given to camouflage to *correct* the figure imbalance. In other words, a cross means correct camouflage is needed, or you should avoid the style altogether. For instance if you have a V neckline hanging in your wardrobe and you have a cross because you have a long neck, you can salvage it by wearing a short necklace or scarf tied high around the neck, or a shirt or camisole underneath.

If your numbers are *not* under a style, then the style is acceptable.

Before we start, it is important to consider the question of the scale, cut and detail of the clothes you wear in relation to your body size.

Scale and You

For your overall look to be effective, the *scale* of your outfit should not overwhelm you, or distract attention from you; it should be in balance and harmony with your figure image. The size of pattern and weight of fabric should be compatible in scale with the garment it is made into, and with the size of the person who is going to wear it.

The numbers on the questionnaire on page 73 are a guideline to your scale.

If you came up small scale and you are over 5′ 5″ you can lean closer to medium scale. If you came up medium scale and your height is over 5′ 5″ you can lean to the direction of large scale. If, on the other hand, you came up large scale and you are under 5′ 5″ tall, you'll have to taper your scale down towards medium.

As a general point, for all scales, it is worth remembering that unless you are exceptionally slender, tight-fitting clothes will emphasise any bulk or bulges. If you are too thin, they will emphasise your bones. Generally speaking, well-cut clothes which have had fabric used generously in their construction, will always hang well and give a better look.

The advice on these pages about the scale of clothes and patterns also holds true for jewellery and accessories. For instance, if you are small scale, you will be overwhelmed by large dangly earrings and a big handbag. Similarly, a large scale person will look wrong with tiny dainty earrings or a minuscule handbag.

SMALL

If you came up with three or more of these numbers – 9, 12, 14, 24 – you have a fine or small bone structure and great care should be taken when purchasing clothing. The line, fabric patterns and detail you choose should be small and light to average in size, giving a fine line.

AVERAGE

If you circled mainly 'B' for balanced, meaning you have an average balanced bone structure, this is what you take into consideration. You should go for average scale in patterns, weight of fabric, line, detail and accessories.

LARGE

If on the other hand, you circled three or more of the numbers 8, 10, 11, 16, 17, 21, 22, 25, you have a larger than average bone structure and you can wear larger than average patterns, lines, weightier fabrics, fashion detail and accessories.

Necklines and Collars

Study and become familiar with the best neckline for you: as necklines are the lines nearest your face, it's best to *continue* the lines of your face – with straight necklines if your face has straight lines, with softer necklines if your face has softer lines. You should also always consider what *other* collar or necklines you will be wearing with an item of clothing, so as to create a unified look. For instance, if you've got a jacket with a rounded collar, a blouse with a pointed collar won't look right – and vice versa.

Peter Pan
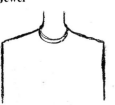
√ 1, 2, 3, 8
× 7

Drape
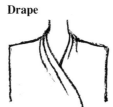
√ 1, 2, 3
× 8

Cowl

√ 1, 2, 3
× 8

Ruffle

√ 1, 2, 3, 8
× 7

Jewel

√ 1, 2, 3, 4, 5, 6, 8
× 7

High Pointed

√ 4, 5, 6, 8
× 7

High Tie

√ 1, 2, 3, 4, 5, 6, 8, 10, 14, 16
× 7

Floppy Bow

√ 1, 2, 3, 8, 10, 14
× 7

Centre Placket
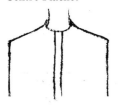
√ 1, 2, 3, 4, 9, 10
× 7

Extended Mandarin

√ 1, 2, 3, 4, 5, 6, 8
× 7

Mandarin
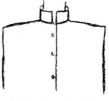
√ 1, 2, 3, 4, 5, 6, 8
× 7

Turtleneck

√ 3, 4, 5, 6, 8
× 7

Figure type	Best points			Worst points		

Heartshape
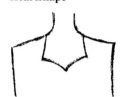

√ 1, 2, 3, 7, 13, 21
× 8, 10, 14

Scoop

√ 1, 2, 3, 7, 21
× 8, 10

V Neck
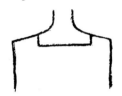

√ 4, 5, 6, 7, 10, 13
× 8, 21

Square
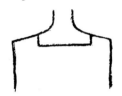

√ 4, 5, 7, 9, 16, 21
× 8, 10, 13

Boatneck

√ 1, 2, 4, 5, 7, 21
× 8, 10

Shawl

√ 1, 2, 3, 7, 10, 15
× 8, 13

Wide Collar

√ 3, 4, 5, 7, 9, 21
× 8, 10

Round Low Collar

√ 1, 2, 3, 7, 10
× 8

Side Notch Lapel

√ 4, 5, 6, 7, 9, 15, 21
× 8

Peaked Lapel

√ 4, 5, 6, 7, 9, 15, 21
× 8, 10

Winged Collar

√ 1, 2, 3, 4, 5, 6
× 10

Chelsea Lapel

√ 4, 5, 6, 7, 10
× 8, 13, 14, 15, 21

* *Some necklines can draw attention where it is not wanted. For instance, the short-waisted should not wear long tie blouses or tops, as the 'ties' bring the eye down to the waist.*

○ If your number is not under a style, then the style is acceptable.	○ A × before your number means that the style draws attention to your figure problem.	○ A √ before your number means a style which suits you and will detract from any figure problem.

Blouses and Tops

These are a woman's best accessory. They can finish off a look by pulling together a skirt and unmatched jacket, or they can be used as a buffer if you choose a colour which will heighten or calm down a not-so-good suit colour. They can also help you to camouflage and disguise a figure problem with their lines, but similarly, if the lines are chosen wrongly, they can draw attention. Those without good waists should not wear their blouses tightly tucked in: the blouse should puff out above the waistband which will disguise the thick waist and they should not wear a draped bodice as that line draws the eye down towards the waist. A straight yoke can actually make broad shoulders look broader.

Straight Yoke

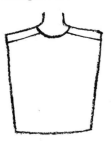

√ 3, 4, 5, 9, 16, 21, 22
× 6, 15

Gathered Yoke

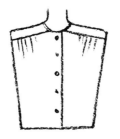

√ 1, 2, 3, 9, 13, 14, 21, 22
× 15

Epaulettes and Shoulder Detail

√ 3, 4, 5, 7, 9, 21, 22
× 10

Bust Pocket or Detail

√ 3, 4, 5, 6, 14, 16
× 13

Peplum

√ 1, 2, 3
× 13, 15, 16, 17, 18, 19, 21, 22, 23

Waist Detail

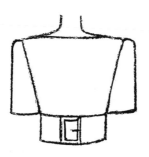

√ 1, 4, 5, 14, 16
× 8, 9, 13, 15, 17, 18, 19, 21

Wrapover Bodice

√ 1, 2, 7, 10, 13, 14, 23
× 8, 9

Belted Tunic Shirt

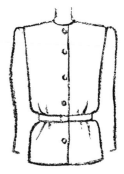

√ 5, 6, 10, 14, 20
× 15, 17, 18, 19, 21, 22, 23

Figure type	Best points			Worst points		
				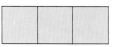		

Shell (worn loose)

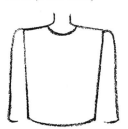

√ 3, 15, 17, 19
× 18, 21

Blouson

√ 3, 10, 13, 14, 15, 16, 17, 20
× 18, 19, 21, 23

Pullover

√ 2, 5, 6, 10, 16, 17, 20
× 18, 19, 21, 23

Sweatshirt

√ 2, 5, 6, 10, 13, 14, 15, 16, 17, 20
× 18, 19, 21, 23

Hipster

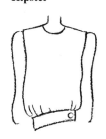

√ 3, 10, 13, 14, 15, 16, 17, 20
× 18, 19, 21, 23

Gathered Yoked Smock

√ 2, 3, 5, 6, 10, 14, 15, 16, 17
× 18, 19, 20, 21, 23

Long Waistcoat

√ 1, 2, 5, 13, 14, 15, 16, 17, 18
× 19, 20, 21, 22, 23

Long Tunic

√ 5, 6, 10, 15, 16, 18, 21
× 22, 23

* *If you want to bring the eye down, choose styles with a centre placket or a tie neckline; if you want to take the eye outwards, choose yokes, square necklines, and shoulder detail. The designs of a fabric – stripes, for instance – can do the same.*

○ If your number is not under a style, then the style is acceptable.

○ A × before your number means that the style draws attention to your figure problem.

○ A √ before your number means a style which suits you and will detract from any figure problem.

81

Skirts

These are so versatile that they can change the look of a jacket from businesslike to dressy or more casual. Make sure the skirts you buy create visual harmony with the detail on your jackets and blouses. Choose the length which is best suited to your legs – fashion needn't dictate to you. If you have wonderful legs, of course, you can wear virtually any length and you can get away with hem detail as well. The most flattering lines in skirts are those which appear longer than they are wide.

Box Pleats

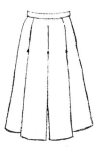

√ 1, 2, 3, 4, 5, 6, 10, 18, 20, 21, 22, 23
× 17, 19

Stitched Pleat

√ 1, 2, 3, 4, 5, 6, 10, 18, 20, 21, 22, 23
× 19

Knife Pleat

√ 1, 2, 3, 4, 5, 6, 10, 17, 18, 20, 21, 22, 23,
× 19

8-Gored/Kilt

√ 4, 5, 6, 10, 17, 21, 22, 23
× 18, 19, 20

Wide Panel

√ 1, 2, 3, 4, 5, 6, 15, 18, 19, 21, 22, 23, 24, 25
× 20

Circular

√ 1, 2, 4, 10, 19, 20, 21, 22
× 17, 18, 24

Dirndl

√ 1, 2, 4, 10, 19, 20, 22
× 17

Trumpet

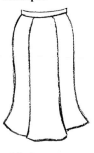

√ 1, 2
× 13, 18, 19, 20, 22

* *Eased straight skirts give a straight skirt look without revealing minor problems.*

* *Flared skirts combine with short and mid-length jackets (between hips and thighs) to create an effective style that can camouflage.*

Figure type	Best points		Worst points	
			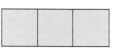	

Straight

√ 5, 6, 23, 24
× 17, 18, 19, 20, 22, 25

Eased Straight

√ 4, 5, 6, 21, 22, 23, 24
× 17, 18, 19, 20, 25

Eased Straight (centre detail)

√ 4, 5, 6, 21, 22, 23, 24
× 17, 18, 19, 20, 25

Low Box Pleats

√ 5, 6, 21, 23, 24
× 17, 18, 19, 20, 22, 25

Tapered

√ 1, 2, 3, 10, 20, 23, 24
× 17, 18, 19, 21, 25

Flared

√ 4, 5, 6, 10, 17, 18, 19, 20, 21, 22, 23, 24, 25

Modified Dirndl with centre detail

√ 1, 2, 4, 5, 10, 17, 18, 19, 20, 21, 22, 23, 24, 25

Culottes

√ 4, 5, 6, 10, 17, 18, 19, 20, 21, 22, 24, 25

* Pleated skirts which are narrow and lie flat can be slimming if your hips are not too wide.

* Always look sideways in a mirror when trying on skirts. Does it hang loose and unrestricted? If not, wear your skirts and waistbands looser to make you look slimmer.

* The heavier the fabric, the bulkier a full skirt looks.

o If your number is not under a style, then the style is acceptable.	o A × before your number means that the style draws attention to your figure problem.	o A √ before your number means a style which suits you and will detract from any figure problem.

Dresses

Choosing dresses which camouflage and take attention away from your not-so-good points emphasises and focuses attention on your good points at the same time. A dress is a top and a bottom together, so what I have already said about necklines, tops and skirts applies here too. Always remember that lines draw the eyes to them, so if you haven't a good waist, avoid waisted dresses; if you've got good hips you *can* happily wear drop-waisted lines. Lengths of dresses again depend on how good your legs are, but I think it's important that you can see some leg if you're supposed to: if a dress is too long, and too little leg is visible, you can look out of proportion.

Fitted Sheath	**Princess Line**	**Double Breasted Coat Dress**

√ 1, 15, 23 × 10, 13, 14, 16, 17, 18, 19, 20	√ 1, 2, 15, 16, 19, 22 × 13, 14, 17, 18	√ 4, 5, 6, 10, 15, 16, 17, 20 × 13, 18, 19

Drop Waisted Dress	**Low Pleats**	**Chemise**

√ 3, 13, 14, 15, 16, 17, 20 × 18, 19, 21, 22, 23	√ 3, 5, 6, 10, 15, 16, 17 × 18, 19, 21, 23	√ 5, 6, 10, 13, 14, 15, 16, 17, 20 × 9, 18, 19, 21, 22, 23, 25

Figure type	Best points			Worst points		

Shift

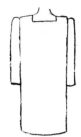

× 14, 18, 19, 21, 22

H. Line

√ 3, 4, 5, 6, 10, 15, 16, 17,
18, 19, 20, 21, 22, 23, 25
× 24

Two Piece

√ 4, 5, 6, 10, 14, 16, 23
× 3, 17, 18, 19, 20, 21

**Draped Bodice Circular
Bottom**

√ 1, 2, 19, 22
× 3, 17, 18

Blouson

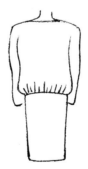

√ 3, 5, 13, 14, 15, 17, 18,
19, 20
× 16, 23

Empire Line

√ 15, 16, 18, 19, 21, 22, 23
× 10, 11, 13, 17

* *A full-skirted dress should never come out further than your shoulders if you're not very tall, as the wider the skirt the shorter you will appear to be.*

* *Always remember to create visual balance between the jackets or coats you will be wearing and your dress.*

○ If your number is not under a style, then the style is acceptable.	○ A × before your number means that the style draws attention to your figure problem.	○ A √ before your number means a style which suits you and will detract from any figure problem.

*T*rousers

The waistband and tops of trousers you choose can help to add curves or even take them away, emphasising slim hips or camouflaging a slightly rounded stomach. For instance, if the pleats or gathers at the waistband face inwards, they're more slimming; if they face outwards, they tend to bulk up on the hips.

TROUSER TOPS

Smooth Waistband

√ 23
× 18, 19, 20, 21, 22

Plain Trouser Top

√ 17, 21
× 18, 19,20

Jean

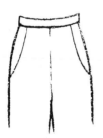

√ 20
× 17, 18, 19, 21, 22

Eased Pleats or Gathers

√ 18, 19, 20, 21 22
× 0

* *The baggier a trouser leg, the shorter you will look. Straight legs are the best all-round trousers.*

* *Wearing trousers allows you to wear longer tops, as the line of the trousers is continuous from waist to foot.*

Figure type	Best points	Worst points

TROUSER LEGS

Straight

√ 19, 20, 21, 22, 23, 24

Tapered Leg

√ 23
× 10, 18, 19, 20, 21, 22, 24, 25

Flared Bottom

√ 23, 24
× 18, 19, 20, 21, 22, 25

Baggy Wide Leg
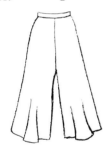

√ 10, 18, 19, 20, 21, 22, 23, 24, 25
× 18, 19, 20

Jodhpur

√ 10, 20, 23
× 18, 19, 21, 22

Gathered

√ 10, 19, 20, 22, 24
× 18

* *Turn-ups shorten the leg, so don't wear them if your legs are short!*

○ If your number is not under a style, then the style is acceptable.	○ **A** × before your number means that the style draws attention to your figure problem.	○ **A** √ before your number means a style which suits you and will detract from any figure problem.

*J*ackets and Coats

Your main pieces of clothing like jackets and coats should be chosen because they combine well, both in colour and style, with other clothing. At the same time they must camouflage your negative areas as well as emphasise the points of your body which are flattering to you. The best all-round jacket is a single breasted, as it goes with most styles of skirts and can be worn with trousers.

Single Breasted Suit

√ 1, 4, 14
× 10, 11, 13, 17, 18, 19, 21

Double Breasted Suit

√ 5, 6, 9, 10
× 13, 17, 18, 19, 21, 22

Short Fitted Jacket

√ 1, 4, 5, 9, 14, 15, 21, 23
× 10, 13, 16, 17, 18, 19

Collarless Fitted Jacket

√ 1, 4, 9, 14
× 10, 11, 13, 17, 18, 19

Unstructured

√ 2, 3, 5, 6, 9, 13, 14, 20
× 4

Blazer

√ 5, 6, 7, 10, 13, 14, 17, 20
× 21

Curved cut away

√ 1, 4, 7, 10, 20, 23
× 13, 17, 19, 21, 22

Single Breasted Cutaway Bottom

√ 2, 4, 5, 7, 10, 14, 20, 23
× 18, 19, 21, 22

* *Good hips? Then end your jackets on your hip line.*

* *Slim thighs? Tapered skirts and jackets bring the eyes to this area.*

* *Never wear jackets that finish at a negative point, unless you have corrected the negative.*

* *Small? Jackets which are cut away at the bottom show more skirt and make you look taller.*

Figure type	Best points	Worst points
		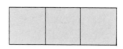

Long Tunic

√ 3, 5, 6, 7, 10, 13, 14, 15, 16, 17, 18, 19, 20
× 23

Chanel

√ 5, 8, 14, 15, 23
× 7, 10, 13, 14, 16, 17, 18, 19, 20, 21, 22

Straight Waist Length

√ 5, 6, 7, 10, 14, 15, 23
× 13, 16, 17, 18, 19, 21, 22

Bolero

√ 1, 2, 7, 10, 14, 16, 23
× 13, 15, 17, 21

Tapered

√ 1, 2, 3, 9, 11, 12, 14, 15, 16, 17, 18, 20, 21, 24
× 10, 22

Car Coat

√ 5, 6, 10, 15, 16, 17, 24
× 9, 13, 18, 19, 21, 22

Edge to Edge

√ 1, 2, 4, 5, 13, 14, 18, 19, 20, 21, 22
× 9

Tuxedo

√ 2, 3, 7, 13, 15, 16, 17, 25
× 9, 10, 18, 19, 20, 21, 22, 24

Chesterfield

√ 3, 5, 6, 10, 15, 16, 17, 24
× 13, 18, 19, 21, 22

Wide Collar (Fitted Waist)

√ 1, 2, 3, 4, 9, 14, 19, 22
× 18, 19, 21

Trench

√ 4, 5, 9, 14, 20, 21, 22
× 10, 13, 15, 16, 17, 18, 19

Wrap

√ 1, 2, 3, 4, 5, 6, 14, 20, 22
× 9, 10, 13, 15, 16, 18, 19, 21

- ○ If your number is not under a style, then the style is acceptable.
- ○ A × before your number means that the style draws attention to your figure problem.
- ○ A √ before your number means a style which suits you and will detract from any figure problem.

Swagger

√ 1, 2, 3, 7, 13, 15, 16, 17,
   18, 19, 20, 21, 22, 25
× 9, 10, 24

Unstructured

√ 5, 6, 9, 11, 13, 14, 15,
   16, 17, 20
× 19, 21, 22

Double Breasted Princess Line

√ 4, 5, 9, 19, 20, 22
× 10, 13, 14, 17, 18

Straight Yoked

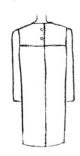

√ 4, 5, 6, 9, 10, 13, 14, 15,
   16, 17, 18, 19, 20
× 21, 22

Curved Yoke

√ 1, 2, 3, 9, 10, 13, 14, 15,
   16, 17, 18, 19, 20, 21
× 7

Stole

√ 1, 2, 3, 11, 12, 14, 15,
   16, 17, 18, 19, 20, 21, 22,
   23
× 9, 10

Straight Long Knitted

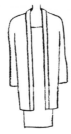

√ 1, 2, 3, 11, 12, 14, 15,
   16, 17, 18, 19, 20, 21, 22,
   23
× 9, 10

Tapered Hem

√ 2, 3, 13, 14, 15, 16, 17
× 9, 19, 21, 22, 25

Sleeves

Make sure your sleeves are wide enough to hang free from the shoulder: if they are big and bulky, or *too* tight, they add unwanted pounds. All body types can wear the set-in sleeve.

Figure type	Best points		Worst points

Set In

√ 1, 2, 3, 4, 5, 6

Raglan

√ 2, 10, 11
× 3, 4, 9, 13, 14, 19, 21, 22

Dolman

√ 6, 12, 21, 22
× 3, 4, 9, 10, 13

Kimono

√ 14, 21, 22
× 9, 10, 12

Capped

√ 5, 21, 22
× 3, 4, 9, 10, 11, 12

Short Puff

√ 1, 9, 14, 21, 22
× 10, 11, 12, 13

Bishop Sleeve

√ 1, 2, 3, 10, 11, 12
× 19, 21, 22

Detailed or Padded Shoulders

√ 9, 11, 17, 21, 22
× 10

Epaulettes

√ 3, 4, 5, 9, 21, 22
× 10

Cuffed

√ 5, 6, 10, 12
× 11, 21, 22

Frilled Cuffs

√ 1, 3, 10, 12
× 11, 21, 22

Short Cuffed

√ 3, 4, 5, 12, 14
× 10, 11, 13

---

* *If you need to extend the shoulderline, choose sleeves wider than the natural bodyline and add shoulder pads to make a smooth unbroken line.*

* *Slim and semi-full looking long sleeves look good on everyone, but a sleeve which is too full can add width, so always be guided by your bone scale.*

○ If your number is not under a style, then the style is acceptable.

○ A × before your number means that the style draws attention to your figure problem.

○ A √ before your number means a style which suits you and will detract from any figure problem.

Pockets and Belts

Pockets work like line, and will attract attention to specific areas, so make sure that if the pocket is visible it is flattering to the area of the body it is drawing attention to. If you have large hips or thighs, you shouldn't have pockets on your hip line. However, pockets can also be *used to draw attention to and camouflage* a possible negative: for instance, someone with little or no bust can happily wear pockets which will make her bust look 'bigger'; the same pockets will camouflage a large bust.

Belts are one accessory that can help you change the mood of your dress – plain leather for business, fancy and elaborate for evening. Wear a colour to coordinate with the top half if you are short waisted, or vice versa if long waisted.

Breast	Just Below Waist	Below Hipline
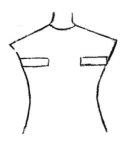		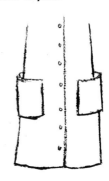
√ 14, 16, 21 × 10, 11, 13	√ 10 × 17, 18, 21, 22	√ 10, 20 × 16, 17, 19, 21, 22

Narrow	High Fitting	Low Fitting
	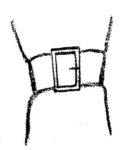	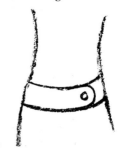
All figures	√ 16 × 13, 15, 17, 18	√ 10, 13, 15 × 16, 18, 19, 20, 21, 23

Figure type	**Best points**			**Worst points**		
				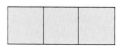		

Broad Sash

√ 18, 21, 23
✕ 10, 16

Hip Belt

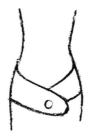

√ 10, 15
✕ 16, 18, 19, 21

Wide Belt

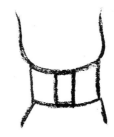

√ 16
✕ 13, 15, 17, 18, 21

Sculptured

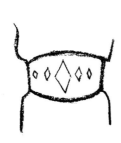

√ 16
✕ 13, 15, 17, 18, 21

Hip Scarf

√ 10, 13, 15
✕ 16, 18, 19, 21

* *Belting your waist to make it look smaller may make your hips look proportionately larger.*

* *To minimise attention to the waist area avoid shiny metal, eye-catching buckles and designs, and different colours.*

○ If your number is not under a style, then the style is acceptable.

○ A ✕ before your number means that the style draws attention to your figure problem.

○ A √ before your number means a style which suits you and will detract from any figure problem.

Shoes and Bags

Your lifestyle will dictate what type of shoes you need in your wardrobe. When buying, look for good quality leather, suede or skin, as they not only look better, they retain their shape better than cheap imitations. Above all, you must buy for comfort, for no matter how great the shoes look, if they're not comfortable, you won't get the amount of wear you should from them.

Always consider what kind of garment the shoes are to be worn with – colour and style – and what sort of conditions you will be wearing them under. A heavy shoe will never look right with a silk or soft looking dress, just as a dressy sandal doesn't go with a serious business suit. Pumps/court shoes in your basic neutrals will go with most suits and dresses.

HANDBAGS

Handbags don't have to match your shoes these days, but they do have to tone, contrast or harmonise with the outfit as a whole. Other important considerations are: In what situation will you need a handbag? Will you be carrying a briefcase? Or anything else? Do you really need to carry round everything except the kitchen sink?

Very structured bags with straight lines are best for figure types 5 and 6, not so structured with gentle straight lines for figures 3 and 4. The floppy, curvier lines should be chosen for figure types 1 and 2 as these go better with your clothes line. Do remember *scale* as well.

USEFUL SHOE SHAPES FOR ALL FIGURE SHAPES

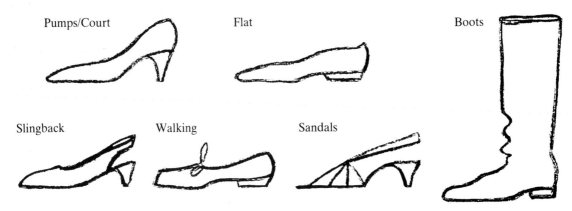

Pumps/Court   Flat   Boots

Slingback   Walking   Sandals

* *A medium heel makes you look taller, at the same time as being more comfortable than the higher, more spectacular styles.*

* *If you are on your feet all day, changing your shoes and height of heel will reduce foot fatigue (which always shows on your face).*

* *When wearing boots, make sure no leg is showing because it cuts the line.*

Figure type	Best points			Worst points		

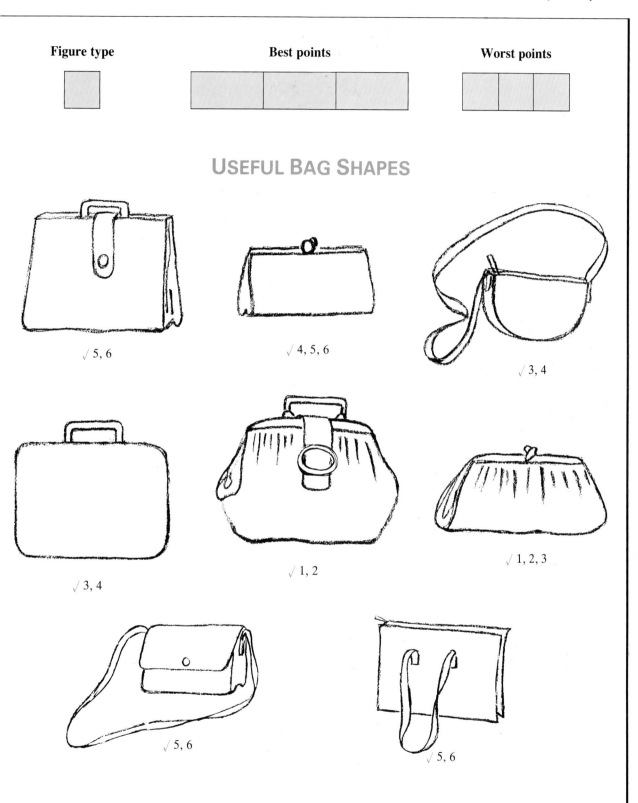

USEFUL BAG SHAPES

√ 5, 6

√ 4, 5, 6

√ 3, 4

√ 3, 4

√ 1, 2

√ 1, 2, 3

√ 5, 6

√ 5, 6

Jewellery

Just as with lines in clothes, choose your jewellery to emphasise your positive points and to draw attention away from your less good points. Buy carefully, too, so that you can mix and match different pieces, just as with clothes.

Gold and pearl earrings, necklaces and pins, for example, are very versatile, and can give you many looks. You can wear them on their own, or mix and match them – a gold or silver chain and pearl necklace, for instance, can be worn singly, or together, or even entwined together for an after-six look. It is very useful to collect pieces which will play double roles – earrings which will double up as pins, or necklaces which will make bracelets (see the illustrations overleaf for ideas). Always use your pieces of jewellery to attract attention. You could wear jewellery on your lapel or on a scarf draped round your shoulders. Point away from your figure faults –

down if you have wide shoulders, up if you have a thick waist. If you have a small waist or hips, wear two earrings side by side there, or on a scarf you have draped around your waist. Last year's hat can be made to look interesting and new with earrings clipped on the hatband, as can your shirt cuffs. Choose the correct *length* of necklaces or chains to match your figure image: in general shorter if you have a long neck, longer if you have a short neck.

Because earrings – which make everyone look 'dressed' – are worn so near the face, they need to be considered very carefully so that they continue the line of the face or flatter it. Not many of us can get away with long dangly earrings, but remember for those who can, that they're not all that suitable for everyday or business wear anyway. Keep them for evenings. Here are some guidelines on choosing the right earrings for your face shape.

ROUND-SHAPED FACE

Choose earrings which give a lift to the face, such as ovals or swirls which are longer than they are wide. Tear drops are flattering, but long dangly earrings which end near the jawline are not good as they shorten and widen the face.

HEART-SHAPED FACE

Choose styles which are broader at the bottom, like pear or triangle shapes or a drop hoop. Dangling earrings can be worn with a really narrow jaw to add width. Shapes which give width near to the ears are not best for you.

OVAL-SHAPED FACE

You have the freedom to choose most shapes and designs.

PEAR-SHAPED FACE

Choose styles which sweep upwards, or are wide at the top and narrow at the bottom. Drop earrings which end near your jawline are taboo as they draw attention to your wide jawline.

RECTANGLE-SHAPED FACE

Choose styles which give width to your long narrow face – square and angled or chunky. Avoid drop earrings as these will make your face look even longer.

OBLONG-SHAPED FACE

As above, but choose softer styles with more curve.

SQUARE-SHAPED FACE

Choose styles which sweep upwards – medium shells, swirls, zig-zag styles. Avoid long dangly earrings which end at the jawline.

DIAMOND-SHAPED FACE

Choose styles which are broader at the bottom – triangle or chandelier shapes. Shapes which give too much width at the ear are not best for you.

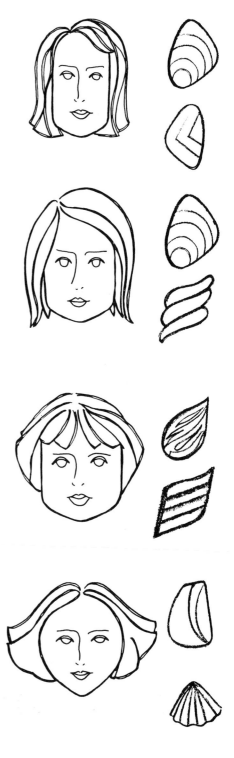

VERSATILE JEWELLERY SHAPES

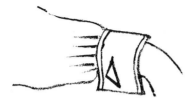

A pair of earrings can double up as cufflinks. (Use *french cuff* fastenings, in other words, put the earring post through both sides of the cuff, so that it will not catch on anything.)

Good waists or hips can be emphasised by wearing two earrings together to make a brooch.

Brooches pinned to a hat add interest.

Twist a plain pearl necklace together with a gold chain for a sophisticated evening look. Try wearing necklaces as bracelets, too.

Earrings can be worn as a scarf pin.

Making the most of your Figure

We all know it's no good trying to fit a square peg into a round hole or vice versa, so why try to fit a straight or angular figure type into clothes which are designed and made with a curved figure in mind. The same goes for clothes which are made for a straight body, they just don't work on a curvy figure without a great deal of adjustment.

PERSONAL STYLE

The surest way to look well dressed is to have a balance of colour, line and fabric, which is in harmony with your figure image. Your clothing feels more comfortable having the same lines as your body and the individual pieces fit together better, making mixing and matching so easy. Think about it. This doesn't mean you have to conform and look like every other woman who happens to have the same figure type as yourself. Far from it. We are all as individual as our fingerprints and should be proud to be so. The aim is to find yourself and project your best self image, not be a copy-cat or clone of some-

one else. You should be delighted that you now know how to be an individual in your own right. Let your clothes express your true self.

The secret of dressing well is knowing what you are doing and why you are doing it. In other words use this book for your reference, study and learn all there is to know about yourself, your colouring, line, lifestyle, likes and dislikes and enjoy yourself. Only then can you develop your own personal style which works for you.

Personal style means liking what you are, and feeling confident and in control. If you don't feel this way yet, don't despair, go through the motions, believe you can do it and you really will start to bring out your full potential. Start being positive about yourself.

The more you see yourself in outfits that are right for you, the happier you will be. Your confidence will grow, this in turn will influence others, making their confidence in you grow as well.

For your best look, you need to select the shapes in clothing that are most flattering to your figure image. These are the main points to look for.

* *Even if you don't have a wonderful face and figure, it doesn't matter. Style is about making the most of what you have.*

* *Remember that 'less is more'. You will find it's best to spend more money on good quality items that you can rely on every time, rather than wasting lots of smaller sums of money on little-worn impulse buys and 'mistakes'.*

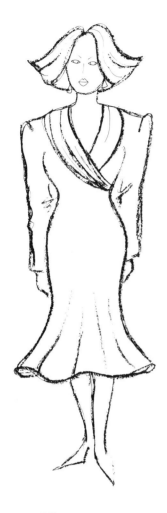

CURVED/HOURGLASS

The hourglass figure is the classic feminine ideal, and can always wear shape, so clothing lines which have some curve suit you best. These, however, should not be too rounded or tight, as this adds unwanted pounds. Use soft shoulder pads that extend your shoulder past the thickest part of your arm, hips or thighs, as this will visually balance the body and prevent fabric clinging and looking too tight. Wear details like yokes, waistline shaping and hemlines to accent your good points. You can usually wear any skirt length which is in style, but you should always consider how appropriate it is for the occasion. Skirts camouflage better than trousers if you are prone to putting weight on around your stomach area. If need be, slacken your waistbands and belts, and avoid tight or excessive fabric below the waist. Wear fabrics which give a sense or feeling of softness, which smooth and drape over your curves revealing your soft line.

Fabric: loosely woven crêpe de chine, crêpe, jersey, jersey wool, crêpe wool, chiffon, raw silk, satin.

Pattern: floral, watercolour, swirl, scroll.

HEART

With a heart body shape, which has a gentle graceful outline, your clothes should follow the same soft curves. You should wear shoulder pads which will help you extend your shoulders past the thickest part of your arm to allow your sleeves to hang unrestricted, or wear raglan sleeves to soften and camouflage. Use designs which bring the eye to the centre: a V or U neckline, vertical stripes or tucks all make the shoulders look narrower, and a high yoke with gathers or a draped bodice are excellent camouflages for the heavy busted person. You can go to extremes with your hemline, very short and flared, to long and flowing, but you should always consider how appropriate your look is for the occasion. Stay clear of fabric which clings and looks too tight; fabrics which smooth and drape are best for you.

Fabric: crêpe wool, jersey, jersey wool, open-weave wool, loosely woven crêpe de chine, crêpe, challis, chiffon, raw silk, and satin.

Pattern: floral, watercolour, swirl, and scroll.

STRAIGHT

You should endeavour to draw the eye away from the waist, at the same time trying to create the illusion of a waist by wearing shoulder pads to give you an extra 1–1½ inches (2.5–4 cm), or create a fullness at the top with yokes or epaulettes. Necklines and collars need to be kept straight, in line with the rest of your body. Wear high or low waisted styles, broad shoulders, unfitted jackets which slope to the waist or just below if under 5′ 4″, to hip or thighs if taller. The slimmer you are the briefer your skirt can be, but you should always consider the appro-priateness of the occasion. Designs and fabric should have a straight feel about them.

Fabric: tightly woven gabardine, linen, twill, silk, Thai silk, taffeta, moiré, satin, polished cotton, piqué.

Pattern: abstract, geometric, sharp, plaid, check, houndstooth, herringbone. Printed or striped fabric on the top half of the body in light or bright colours with a solid colour on the bottom half will create balance.

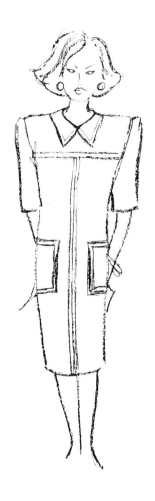

ANGULAR

Your body is angular without curves. Straight clothing lines are a natural extension of your body line – classic shirt notched collars, long cuffed sleeves. You should use fabric and designs which are straight in line and feel. You can wear fullness and/or horizontal lines at the hip and hemline to offset and balance the width above. Styles with vertical lines at the top ending in a full skirt, hip line pockets, dropped waists, long jackets which are straight or slightly tapered towards the hemline, are good. Skirt lengths can go to extremes – very short and flared to long and flowing. The appropriateness of the occasion should always be considered.

Fabric: tightly woven gabardine, linen, polished cotton, twill, silk, Thai silk, taffeta, satin, moiré.

Pattern: abstract, geometric, plaid, check, herringbone, houndstooth.

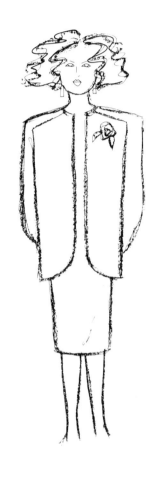

ELLIPSE

You have a little more flexibility, and you can lean either way. The bustier types usually lean to slightly curved necklines, and the little or no bust to the slightly straight. Short necks wear necklines and collars low, while long necks wear them high. Your shoulders need a great deal of attention and you should endeavour to balance them from the front and side views. You will always need shoulder pads to look balanced. A straight yoke, wider collars and lapels all help to visually broaden the shoulders. Wear blouse and dress designs which take attention away from your waistline and taper to emphasise your hips, thighs or hemline, whichever is the best.

Fabric: (gently woven) For a gentle look you will need fabrics which smooth and drape – jersey, crêpe de chine, crêpe, crêpe wool, challis, chiffon, raw silk and satin. For a straight look add linen, thai silk, tweed, wool and flannel.

Pattern: For a gentle look – floral, watercolours, swirl and scroll; for a straight look – add paisley, plaid check and tweed.

PEAR

You have gentle and straight lines to your body and your clothes should be the same. Always wear shoulder pads which will make your shoulders look broader than the thickest part of your body, and line designs which broaden the top half of your body. Straight yokes, wider collars and lapels are for you. Horizontal lines all add width. The hips and thighs need to look narrower. To achieve this visual balance, use centre interest on your bottom half such as buttons or centre pleat, or A-line skirts with vertical lines of buttons down the centre. Your best skirt length is just below the knee to mid calf.

Fabric: loosely woven linen, Thai silk, challis, tweed, satin, jersey, wool flannel, raw silk.

Pattern: paisley, plaid, check, tweed, houndstooth.

Creating an Illusion

Over the years I have met thousands of girls who are not happy with their bodies: the fat want to be thin, the skinny want to be fatter, the tall and lanky want to be shorter, and the short want to be taller, etc. In almost every case, to achieve success and to create the right role for themselves, they have to make the most of what they have now and not wait for something which may never happen, fat becoming slim for instance. But they can *work* on what they have, and I have found that once they have used colour, line and style cleverly, they will look slimmer or heavier as the case may be.

BIG AND BOUNTIFUL

If you are a big lady, why not try to be the most attractive big lady in town? Working at losing weight isn't the question here – you can still create a few illusions and add some colour to your life. Black is thought to be slimming, but it's not always. Even though I consider it a good neutral, not everyone wears it equally well (see page 40–1), and too much of it can be boring. Imagine someone who is big, dressed all in black against a pale background in your home or office. The black will create a big contrast, and will be *more noticeable* than a medium intensity colour from her colour band. That doesn't mean that big girls should never wear black, but they should break it up, creating interest by using colour and line combinations, as well as all the details already given for their figure image.

SHORT BIG GIRLS

Always remember that a horizontal line, whether created by a colour break or a line design, is shorten-ing, adds width, and attracts attention. Bulky fabric adds width as well, and can visibly shorten your look. Very full skirts can also add weight as they pull the eye down.

The following suggestions will make you look visibly taller and slimmer.

1.   Use all one colour, one of your best neutrals, for shoes, tights and suit or dress, or add a contrast colour at the neckline, or create a contrasting centre panel, or detail with buttons.
2.   Still keeping shoes, tights, dress or suit in one of your best neutrals, add a multi-coloured blouse in your best basic colours.
3.   Have your shoes, tights and dress in the same colour, and wear a contrast colour in the jacket, cardigan or coat.

TALL BIG GIRLS

If you are in this category, you have the advantage of being able to bring more mixes of colour to your look, but you should still be careful not to end one colour and start a contrast colour in a place which can't stand to be scrutinised. Colour and line design draw other people's eyes and grab their attention. Also keep your figure image in mind. Break up your line with your tights – these should contrast in light to medium neutral shades – and wear shoes the same intensity as or darker than your hemline.

You can create an illusion of being shorter and smaller by some of the following.

1.   Break up your line by wearing a bright colour combination on the top half, and one of the colours from the top as a block colour for the bottom.

2.   A one-piece dress with a big collar in a contrast colour extending down the middle is visually slimming.

3.   A big yoked, one-coloured seven-eighths jacket which tapers slightly towards hemline over a multi-coloured dress or suit is visually very flattering.

TALL AND SKINNY

Girls who are tall and skinny can have just as many hang-ups as short and plump girls, but visual balance soon sorts them out. Colour breaks and horizontal lines in the cut of your clothes, patterns and colour, all help to give them width. To create the illusion of having a bust, use horizontal lines in design and fabric, yokes with gathers, breast pockets and loose cross-over designs. (Some lines work both ways, and these styles can help one *camouflage* a big bust.) Use shoulder pads to help create a waist. Bulky fabric for skirts or big unstitched folds from the waist band, all add shape to this figure. Wear double-breasted jackets, big belts with interesting buckles, and light to medium neutral tights to create a break in colour between shoes and hemline.

The following will also help.

1.   A check or patterned suit incorporating some of the above lines.

2.   Wear a multi-coloured or horizontal striped top to create breaks, and add a contrasting belt or shoes.

3.   You could wear a pleated plaid or check skirt with one of its colours taken up in a blouse, and another picked up in the jacket, belt and shoe colour.

JUST SHORT

Most people know that using one colour – preferably a dark one – from head to foot can make you look taller and slimmer, and that the use of vertical lines helps the illusion. However, here are a few more hints and tips. Always avoid breaking up colour and line horizontally and wearing a bulky fabric, as this can further shorten your image.

1.   Wear one colour from neck to toe.

2.   Matching tights to shoes and hemline will elongate your legs. Choose from your neutral colours for day, use the other colours for evening.

3.   Wearing colours which are close in colour value will help you appear taller.

4.   Wear a garment all in one colour (like a suit or a coat), with matching tights and shoes and blouse in contrasting colour.

5.   Match shoes and tights colours to the inside colour – a dress or matching skirt and blouse. Use a contrast colour for a long or short coat, and combine the dress colour and coat colour by adding a toning pocket handkerchief, jewellery and scarf.

PART FOUR

WARDROBE
CONFIDENCE

You will find that creating your own style is really very simple and will come naturally with your new-found confidence about colour, your figure, and which lines in clothes suit you best. However, every six months the fashion designers show off their latest creations, and many of us feel very tempted to follow their lead. Well, if you have the time, money and inclination to change your wardrobe twice a year and you know exactly what will work for you and what will not, then by all means go ahead, but I suspect that many of us will lack the time and money that the 'dedicated follower of fashion' requires.

So, if we don't want to get caught up in this six-monthly merry-go-round, what options are we left with? Let's get one thing straight from the start. Just because a style is in fashion, it doesn't mean that everyone is going to look fantastic in it. So if the new fashion trend this season is on your negative figure image list (see pages 74–93), then forget it. You alone should now be able to dictate your unique fashion look, not a designer who has never seen you or considered your figure type.

Your clothes should say something about you. They should tell the world that you are in charge, that you know your own body and how to dress it to look your best. You can lean in a fashionable *direction* but your appearance should always be kept in check by applying all the 'rules' you have already learned, and those that you will encounter in the next few pages. The 'classic' look in fashion is one that I would recommend as the most useful to build your wardrobe around: from a clothes point of view, classic style is characterised as simple balanced form, with regular cut, fit and style, which is not subject to the dictates of the fashion industry and seasonal changes. Wear it in your own unique way, and you will radiate confidence.

Looking and Acting the Part

I am convinced that we are judged on first impressions, and that how we look and act speaks volumes about us before even a word is spoken. Your clothes and grooming receive an instant reaction, and so often there is no second chance to correct a misconception. It is therefore vital to learn the language of clothing, and to communicate successfully with it.

I know that we are always judged by the clothes we wear. Surely not, I hear you say, but we are, and what's more, *you* judge *others* in the same way. Think about it.

▌ Projecting the Right Image

Imagine for a moment that I was the teacher in a class you had just enrolled in to learn about colour, style and wardrobe planning. You arrive on the first day, all eager to learn, and I turn up in tatty jeans and a sloppy sweater, without any make-up on and without bothering to camouflage my pear-shaped body. What would your first impression be? That you had somehow got into the wrong class? Or that I didn't know much about colour and style? My level of knowledge would not be diminished because of how I looked, but that crucial first impression would have put questions in your mind about my ability to teach the subject or do a good job.

If we turn that idea round, how do you think I would feel if I were dressed that way, knowing I had to meet new people, and gain their confidence in my ability to teach. A mammoth task, if you consider that I was clearly showing, by what I was wearing, that I didn't have enough confidence in my own ability to dress well. I would be showing that I lacked self-esteem and that I need not be taken seriously. To cite a real-life example of this, I was recently talking about this very subject to the chief executive of an international company. He told me that just that week the company had not appointed one of their existing staff to a vacant high position. This wasn't because he wasn't capable or didn't have the proper qualifications (he had more than the necessary), but because he didn't *look the part*, and would not have represented the company image they wished to project.

▌ Feeling Confident

If how you look is important, so is how you act. To reinforce that image of confidence (to which your carefully chosen clothes contribute), you can learn a simple method of really feeling, as well as projecting confidence and inner tranquillity.

I was painfully shy when young, because I was an only child, with less than four years' formal education, and had been brought up to speak only when I was spoken to, and never to speak to strangers. Later in my business life, I *had* to speak to strangers and make conversation, putting over a presentation and winning their confidence, and the thought really terrified me. So before every single meeting, I used to *visualise* in my head every single possible circumstance: I would visualise walking in, holding out my hand and introducing myself, and go through the whole situation step by step in my mind, right up to the successful conclusion of the meeting. Because of this mental role-playing, I never now have a problem, and that once shy girl was able to give a talk in August 1981, in San Francisco, California, to 3,000 executives. It was a resounding success. You can do the same. Just remember always to PLAN, PREPARE and VISUALISE what you are going to WEAR, SAY and DO.

Matching your Wardrobe to your Lifestyle

The vast majority of women have a far more complex lifestyle than men, as they are constantly juggling their time between work, home, children, cooking, social life and leisure activities.

It is generally true that when it comes to running their own lives, women are highly organised in their approach. Often they are far more organised than men, because they have to divide their time so carefully between work, and caring for a home and family. Yet even if they manage their own lives extremely well, they rarely devote these skills to managing their wardrobes successfully. This diversity of roles played by women today demands an equally diverse choice of clothes, yet most of us buy on impulse. Our wardrobes bulge at the seams, with nothing that matches or goes with anything else.

▪ Running Your Wardrobe

By building on the confidence you will already have acquired concerning your figure and your best colours and styles, I should now like to help you learn how to prune your existing wardrobe and choose other articles of clothing for a wardrobe that will work uniquely for you.

First of all, a careful examination of your diary for the past twelve months will enable you to gauge how your waking hours were spent. (We always tend to think that most of these will be at work, but in fact by adding up hours in the evening and the two days of the weekend, the average person actually spends more time *away* from work.) Assessing how many hours, days, weeks etc. were spent on your different activities, work, play, and social life, will lead you to realise where the largest or the smallest proportion of your clothes allowance should be spent, assuming that the next twelve months will be spent in much the same way. If you know in advance that they will not be, then naturally you can make adjustments. In either case, you will have a starting point for managing your wardrobe and your budget.

It is when you are at work, of course, that 'looking the part' is most important, and it is your 'career wardrobe' that should be your first consideration – and, in some senses, the easiest. (You'll find some rough guidelines on the next few pages.) But planning your after-business wardrobe can be much more complex, when you have to try to visualise each situation – collecting the children from school, entertaining your business colleagues or your husband's, going to the theatre, having a quiet drink in a wine bar, or simply relaxing in front of the TV. In any situation, the essential thing is always to select clothes for their appropriateness, comfort and ability to give you confidence.

▪ Wardrobe Planning

I have divided types of work into four categories, and non-work activities into two. Deciding which category your lifestyle comes under is the first step in planning a successful wardrobe. Doing this will help you realise the demands which are most likely to be placed on your wardrobe. By learning how to stage-manage, manipulate, adjust and accommodate your wardrobe to different situations, you will not only be prepared for any eventuality, but you will be able to add your own individual touch with ease and confidence. Just write down the letter of the category you spend most time in, then the ones which come second and third in the Personal Profile on page 126.

A THE CORPORATE PROFESSIONS

The term 'corporate' describes those amongst you who work in the city, the law, the civil service, agency work, or any job in which you are representing your company or department, and in which you are expected to look smart and 'conform' as far as clothes are concerned.

The corporate woman used to be restricted to the ultra-conservative business suits and shirts and felt that in order to be a success, she needed to dress as a 'token male'. However, this is no longer the case, as those days of boardroom dressing are gone (and were more aptly described as boredom dressing). You may of course *suit* this kind of look – the straights among you, for instance, will probably feel at home, but other figure types may have felt uncomfortable or ill at ease. Now you have the freedom to learn the delights of 'non-corporate' dressing, and conforming and losing your individuality is a thing of the past. Executive women are beginning to say, 'I know who I am, I am confident about my ability and talent, and I don't have to wear a tie and carry a man's briefcase to prove I can adapt to the corporate role!'

The corporate or executive woman can make her own individual style, provided she still fits the overall picture required by her chosen career path. This new self expression means daring to wear beautiful unmatched suits, separates with a fashionable unblazer-like jacket, or even a well-tailored dress or two-piece dress with or without a jacket, in colours and styles that are flattering as well as business-like. Women are now beginning to learn that being feminine can be an asset if it is coupled with competence and personal flair.

Remember that colour can also give an outfit an authoritative look just as well as style. So choosing classic clothes for your figure image, in the darker neutrals from your tonal group, and in the fabrics suggested for you, will give you a smart executive look. Individualise it by adding blouses in beautiful fabrics in your light neutrals and basic colours. For dress and jacket ensembles, colours are best chosen from your dark neutrals or basic colours; your accessories will do the rest.

▌ Three Suggested Wardrobes

The basis of these wardrobes would be composed of either three matching suits, or matching separates which make up the same classic design. Choose them in the darkest neutrals from your tonal group. Look for good quality fabrics that are preferably composed mainly of natural fibres. If you choose a light – or cool – wool from your clothing line recommendations (see pages 100 to 106), you will be able to wear it throughout most of the year. For warm weather, choose a suit in a blend of silk/wool, silk/linen or silk/cotton.

1. 3 jackets, 3 skirts, 4 blouses, 2 dresses
2. 4 jackets, 4 skirts, 4 blouses
3. 3 jackets, 3 skirts, 4 blouses, 1 two-piece dress

Carefully chosen in your best neutrals and accent colours, these garments will make a surprisingly large number of outfits.

Opposite: *In the top picture, Lisa is wearing her black suit, which forms the basis of her corporate wardrobe. She has given the classic suit a highly individual look by teaming it with a striking yellow sweater and yellow-based scarf which flatter her Dark/Bright look. In the photograph below left, she has combined the skirt of the black suit with a matching black/white silk jacket and white/black top which gives an elegant appearance, suitable for the office but which could carry her through to evening. In the photograph below right, she has teamed the skirt with a vibrant multi-coloured jacket and black camisole, a very dressy outfit suitable for an evening party*

Page 114: *The grey-green suit (top photograph) is an excellent basis for a working wardrobe. The jacket teamed with trousers (below right) is suitable both for work and casual use, and the jacket with kilt (below left) makes a smart casual outfit.*

B THE PEOPLE PROFESSIONS

This covers all of you who work in any sort of business involving communications, whether it's journalism, politics, public relations, social work, teaching, secretarial work – even acting or TV announcing!

The woman who works in communications-related fields has always had more freedom of dress and expression than her executive sister, but that doesn't mean it makes choosing clothes any simpler. Whilst her executive counterpart might have felt bored and restricted by the old stiff and starchy look of her profession, she at least had definite guidelines. The communicator's role can be so varied that she often lacks direction, not being quite sure what is appropriate or acceptable for the task ahead. Her career path takes her into many roles in the people business – meeting the general public in a one-to-one situation, putting her points across to a mass audience in a large hall or in front of a camera, or giving a presentation.

If you are in this business, the clothes you choose should never be severe, stiff or starchy. On the other hand, you have to be very careful not to look *too* casual and non-credible. Every career woman should have at least one matched suit in her wardrobe, but unmatched jackets and skirts are still appropriate and professional for your look. Always think of the individual day ahead, and dress accordingly.

■ Three Suggested Wardrobes

Build your wardrobe around your light to medium neutrals for the main items. Wearing the bright colours from your tonal group – red, blue, green and turquoise – can play a great part in holding the attention of your audience, and will lift those neutrals. Use them in blouses, scarves, etc. Light colours on their own fade into the background, and dark colours look too sombre. Keep your best neutrals and softer shades for your friendly, relaxed look, which people will find easy to approach.

1. 2 jackets, 4 skirts, 1 dress, 4 blouses, 1 sweater
2. 2 jackets, 1 dress, 3 skirts, 4 blouses, 2 sweaters
3. 2 jackets, 4 skirts, 5 blouses, 1 sweater

Carefully chosen in your neutrals and best accent colours, these wardrobes of twelve garments each can combine and make a surprisingly large number of looks.

C THE CARING OR SERVICE PROFESSIONS

In many careers in caring or service, the question of what should be worn today just doesn't have to be given a thought, other than is it clean and well pressed. People like police officers, traffic wardens, air hostesses, nurses and many hotel and restaurant personnel have to wear a uniform at work.

Because their choice of clothes has been taken away from them for a large part of the day, people in this business sometimes lack imagination when it comes to planning a wardrobe for their leisure hours. You should look at sections E and F – leisure – and build a wardrobe around the suggestions.

Page 115: *The pink and blue striped jumper and blue skirt (top photograph) make a comfortable and attractive weekend ensemble. They form the basis for a number of looks. Team the matching cardigan with matching casual trousers (below left) or the skirt with an easy-to-wear sweatshirt for a fun look (below right).*

Opposite: *In the top picture, Barbara is wearing the red suit which forms the basis of her working wardrobe for the People Profession. In the photograph below left, she combines the jacket from her basic suit with a red and white blouse and skirt which can either be worn as a dress as shown here, or teamed with other separates for different looks. In the photograph below right, she has teamed the jacket with a blue checked skirt and white polo neck sweater for a more casual weekend look.*

D THE CREATIVE PROFESSIONS

This category covers businesses such as advertising, publishing, fashion, hairdressing, design, art, branches of the media and music. In all of these fields a certain freedom of expression in dress is accepted. (An accounts executive in advertising or a fashion buyer might lean towards category A.)

As a creative person you need clothes which are comfortable, relaxed and individual. You want to be at ease with yourself, so you can concentrate on the subject or creative situation you are involved in at the time. Yet, on the other hand, you must also *express* your creative ability in your appearance. (Sometimes you can get so involved with the project in hand that you don't think about yourself, for example your lipstick or hair.) Wardrobe planning does not detract from your creativity: it just adds a little helping hand.

Putting your look together with interesting layers and textures comes easily to you. Sometimes this creative arty look can, like the executive look, be off-putting in some respects, and put a barrier between you and other professions. If you need to get onto their wavelength, go for a classic look with some uniquely creative touches, a look that will take you anywhere. Otherwise, you can really be as fashionable and flamboyant as your figure image will allow.

■ Three Suggested Wardrobes

There should be enough basics here so that you can mix and match, with scope for you to add some inspired creativity in mixing textures and layers. As for colour, mix neutrals together, and brights together, for interesting looks.

1. 1 jacket, 2 skirts, 2 pairs of trousers, 3 dresses, 4 tops
2. 2 jackets, 2 skirts, 2 pairs of trousers, 3 blouses, 2 sweaters, 1 dress
3. 2 jackets, 3 skirts, 1 pair of trousers, 2 blouses, 4 sweaters

E SOCIAL LIFE

This will include all those occasions when you want to look quite smart, and although you could have an entirely *separate* wardrobe for going to cocktail parties, balls etc., you could cleverly add to and adapt your career wardrobe for most occasions.

If you're going to the theatre after work, or out for a meal or drink, then a quick freshen up with a change to a more glamorous blouse or jacket, or both, and a different pair of shoes (a change of height refreshes your feet!), with some glamorous accessories, can make your career wardrobe infinitely adaptable. Be as imaginative as possible when selecting these extra items, mixing and matching colours, and combining fabrics cleverly: think of what you could do with a colourful jacket, a satin collar or taffeta bow, a pretty scarf or some glittery costume jewellery.

■ Three Suggested Wardrobes

You should have enough here to carry you through most social activities, both formal and less formal. It isn't necessary to spend a lot of money on new outfits; older ones can be transformed by the cunning use of costume jewellery (see page 99).

1. 2 skirts, 2 pairs of trousers, 2 jumpers, 2 cardigans, 2 silk blouses, 2 camisoles
2. 2 pairs of trousers, 2 skirts, 2 camisoles, 2 silk blouses, 1 evening sweater, 1 dress, 2 jackets
3. 2 evening skirts, 1 pair of evening trousers, 2 camisoles, 2 silk blouses, 2 evening sweaters, 1 evening wrap, 1 jacket with matching top

F SPORT AND LEISURE

Maybe you may fill your leisure time by gardening, doing exercises, or going for walks or simply relaxing at home. Or are you the sporty type who goes riding, swimming, sailing or whatever? If you're a sports enthusiast you'll need clothes that are practical and comfortable, and indeed will almost certainly need specialised clothing for your particular type of sport.

If you feel at home in this sporty, casual look – and many non-working women do – then you'll have to work quite hard at not looking *too* casual or sloppy.

■ Three Suggested Wardrobes

Use your newly acquired colour and style principles to coordinate your casual look, but change some or all of your blouses and skirts for tee-shirts and trousers or tracksuit type attire. Accessories and shoes should be suitable as well; obviously you can't do something like teaming court shoes with a tracksuit bottom. Try to be aware of which fabrics you can and cannot mix and match successfully. For further ideas, turn to pages 100 to 106, and page 120.

1. 2 tracksuits, 3 tee-shirts, 3 sweatshirts, 2 sweaters, 1 jumpsuit, 1 cardigan
2. 2 tracksuits, 2 pairs of trousers, 3 tee-shirts, 2 sweatshirts, 2 sweaters, 1 cardigan
3. 1 tracksuit, 2 pairs of culottes, 3 tee-shirts, 2 sweaters, 1 pullover, 2 blouses, 1 cardigan

Planning a Wardrobe

As you now know, the secret of a wardrobe that works lies in successful coordination and mixing and matching. This may seem obvious, but I wonder how many of the items hanging in your wardrobe truly coordinate with everything else? As I have already mentioned, it's not just a case of combining colours – styles and fabrics have to be considered as well.

STYLE

A wardrobe which is built around classic styles, with good cut, fit and fabric, should last for many years. It is always best to avoid extreme fashion trends. Change hemlines to lean towards a trend if you can, or use accessories to make fashion statements.

Always choose pieces for your coordinated wardrobe which look good together style wise. A single-breasted jacket, for instance, is the best to buy in a suit, as it goes with most styles of skirt, and can be worn with trousers. A double-breasted jacket can look unharmonious with some skirts, and can have the effect of making many small people look plumper and even smaller. There are hints on this in the style section beginning on page 75.

FABRICS

Not all fabrics can be successfully combined, so this is yet another consideration to bear in mind when planning your wardrobe coordination. Pieces which will be worn together must be compatible in weight and texture as well as fibre. All types of wool can be combined – wool flannel with wool crêpe, wool gabardine with wool tweed – but with wool and silk combinations you have to be more careful, and take the weave and weight into consideration. For instance, a lightweight wool gabardine or wool crêpe jacket could be worn over a silk garment, but a heavier wool or tweed just would not work. Silk and linen can be combined, as can linen and cotton, and dressier cottons and silks. Instinct and common sense should help you here!

COLOUR

To look your best, you obviously want to choose your best colours from amongst your tonal groups fans. In most cases, the darker neutrals would be the best for the main basics of your coordinated wardrobe, with your best colours brought in as accents. These colours must all harmonise – the colours with the neutrals, and the colours with each other – for successful ultimate combination. (Look at the colour wheels again to remind yourself about complementary and related colours.) Don't forget either to think about the *psychology* of colour, choosing your wardrobe colours to project the image you want, or what you feel.

THE VERSATILE BASICS

The basis of any working woman's wardrobe will be one of her major purchases, a matching suit. If you are an executive woman (category A) you will probably need at least two suits, and these should preferably be in your best neutrals. If work and lifestyle permit, however, your suit could be your best basic colour – those whose first colour characteristic is bright, for instance, could happily get away with a bright-coloured suit. Both suits should harmonise with each other in style, fabric and colour, because you're going to swap the skirts and jackets around in different combinations.

A similarly versatile purchase could be a tailored, button-through dress, which you can wear jackets over, or shirts under, or a two-piece dress, which will immediately give you several looks in one if you wear the pieces together or separately with other pieces.

The next essential buy is several blouses. These are a woman's best accessory. Buy them with necklines that flatter your figure image (see page 78); this is essential because they're worn close to your face. Be sure to select blouses in your very best colours which will also combine well with the suits. Choose the blouses in a variety of solid colours, with a couple in a pattern, stripe or print; these will give you a tremendous variety of looks. Long sleeves are more dressy and will give a more professional look.

When you can afford to, add extra skirts, trousers and casual leisure wear, depending on the requirements of your lifestyle. This will immediately extend the mixing and matching possibilities of your basic wardrobe. For evening or for your social life after work, you can add silky tops and camisoles in the jewel colours which will transform the career look into the more glamorous. Another vital basic is a smartly tailored coat or raincoat in a quality cloth; choose this in a good neutral that will coordinate with everything else.

THE BASIC ACCESSORIES

For work, you should have at least two pairs of court shoes in a neutral or darker intensity than your hemline (this is particularly important for those who are shorter than average). For social occasions, one pair of sling-back courts can transform the day look into night. For a sporty lifestyle, choose suitable footwear. Tights or stockings should always be chosen to match hemlines and shoes.

For working and travelling, it's a good idea to have one or two small leather shoulder pouch bags in a neutral shade, matching your shoes if you like. This will hold your money, credit cards, make-up etc., and can be fitted under your coat to avoid the horrors of having it snatched. This type of bag will also take you from day to night, and fit into your briefcase.

Select belts in at least two main colours of your wardrobe, and perhaps a couple more in accent colours. Choose them to suit your figure image although in general thin belts are the most versatile.

Scarves can be very useful. Choose at least two medium sized squares or oblongs, and in your best colours to complement the colours in your wardrobe. One could be plain, one discreetly patterned with the coordinating colours. Worn with flair, a beautiful scarf will add the finishing touch to many outfits.

The role of jewellery in a coordinated wardrobe is often underestimated. Pearl earrings and a necklace look discreet during the day, but adding a gold chain to your strand of pearls at night will totally transform the look. Gold or silver chains and earrings are very versatile, and you could add a brooch or bracelet in the same metal. But, please remember, only combine earrings/brooch/watch or bracelet *or* earrings/necklace/watch or bracelet. If you try to wear too much jewellery, you will look very cluttered, and this will only detract from a businesslike image. Individual pieces of jewellery certainly do not need to be real gold, silver, pearls, or whatever (there is a lot of very attractive costume jewellery available nowadays) but it does need to be combined harmoniously for your best look. For example, don't try to wear tiny delicate earrings with a huge chunky brooch, or a thin neckchain with an outsize bracelet! For further ideas on how to wear jewellery, turn to pages 96 to 99.

A Practice Run

To show you how to build up your basic wardrobe, I've done a wardrobe plan for an imaginary client, Mary Jones. She's already filled in a form to allow me to see at a glance all her details – her job and lifestyle, her colour characteristics, her figure image, best and worst points etc.

For her primary lifestyle category which is B, the People Profession, I've chosen twelve basic pieces. In reality, because of the suits and two-piece dress, when mixed and matched this wardrobe will give her more than 60 different looks (see opposite).

For her social life – category E – I've added some silk blouses and camisoles which will combine with the dress, trousers or long skirt, depending on the occasion. These can be coordinated with the career clothes (B) to give even more combinations.

For category F – the sport and leisure time – I've added tee-shirts and comfortable tracksuits and jumpsuits which are ideal for travelling in and for spending time with her family. All these are in coordinating colours and can be mixed with several of the items in the first two categories. I've also added basic accessory lists which will finish off all her outfits.

I have achieved a tremendous variety of looks for this by using mainly wardrobe plan clothes that were already hanging in her wardrobe – the diversity of looks potentially available from the articles of clothing listed here will inspire you and show you how to do the same with your own wardrobe.

As Mary is a Bright, I chose one of her favourite basic colours – red – from her tonal group for the first matching suit, and used one of her best neutrals – ivory or soft white – for her second. If, as an example, I just describe how using one jacket, the red one, can make many different looks, you will understand how the principles of clever wardrobe coordination work.

▪ A Wardrobe Based On A Red Jacket For A 'Bright'

1. Red jacket (buttoned up), red skirt = 1 look
2. Red jacket, red skirt and each of 5 blouses (including the two-piece dress top) = 5 looks
3. Red jacket, ivory skirt and each of 5 blouses = 5 looks
4. Red jacket, two-piece dress, with or without the white blouse = 2 looks
5. Red jacket, two-piece dress skirt, with white blouse = 1 look
6. Red jacket, grey skirt, and each of 5 blouses = 5 looks
7. Red jacket, navy skirt and each of 5 blouses = 5 looks
8. Red jacket, navy and white houndstooth skirt, and each of 3 (plain and houndstooth) blouses = 3 looks
9. Red jacket, navy dress = 1 look
10. Red jacket, navy dress, and each of 5 blouses underneath = 5 looks

There are over 30 looks here based on the same red jacket, in the one category alone, and if you then do the same with the ivory jacket overleaf, you can see what an interesting choice of combinations Mary will have at her disposal! Using the belts, shoes, scarves and jewellery can effect alternative transformations as well.

Opposite is the wardrobe plan for Mary Jones. When you have studied this and seen how it works, you can start planning your own wardrobe on page 126.

CAREER B

1. Matching suit (jacket/skirt)	RED
2. Matching suit (jacket/skirt)	IVORY
3. Two-piece dress	RED AND IVORY HOUNDSTOOTH
4. Skirt	GREY
5. Skirt	NAVY
6. Skirt	NAVY AND WHITE HOUNDSTOOTH
7. Blouse	SOFT WHITE
8. Blouse	EMERALD TURQUOISE
9. Blouse	WHITE WITH BLUE STRIPE
10. Blouse	RED, WHITE, GREY AND NAVY PATTERN
11. Tailored coat dress	NAVY
12. Big coat or mac	NAVY

SOCIAL E

1. Two-piece dress	NAVY AND IVORY PATTERN
2. Long skirt	NAVY
3. Trousers	SOFT WHITE
4. Trousers	NAVY
5. Silk, button-through blouse	SOFT WHITE
6. Silk, button-through blouse	HOT TURQUOISE
7. Silk camisole	SOFT WHITE
8. Silk camisole	HOT TURQUOISE

SPORT AND LEISURE F

1. Jumpsuit	PERIWINKLE
2. Tracksuit	GREY
3. Tee-shirt	YELLOW
4. Tee-shirt	GREEN
5. Jumper/sweater	RED
6. Cardigan coat	GREY, RED AND GREEN PATTERN

ACCESSORIES FOR CAREER B

1. Plain belt	NAVY
2. Plain belt	RED
3. 1 pair plain pumps/courts	NAVY
4. 1 pair plain pumps/courts	GREY
5. 1 pair plain pumps/courts	RED
6. 1 pair earrings	PEARL

ACCESSORIES FOR CAREER   B (cont)

7.	1 pair earrings	GOLD
8.	1 necklace	GOLD
9.	1 brooch	GOLD
10.	1 handbag	IVORY
11.	1 handbag	NAVY
12.	1 briefcase	GREY
13.	1 scarf	MULTI-COLOURED, RED GREY, NAVY, WHITE, GREEN, GEOMETRIC.
14.	1 scarf	MULTI-COLOURED, RED, NAVY, WHITE, CHECK.
14.	Tights	NAVY
15.	Tights	GREY
16.	Tights	FLESH

ACCESSORIES FOR SOCIAL   E

1.	Evening belt	IVORY
2.	1 pair court shoes	IVORY
3.	1 pair strap sandals	NAVY
4.	1 pair earrings	DIAMOND
5.	1 necklace	PEARL
6.	Evening wrap	NAVY
7.	Evening scarf	NAVY, IVORY, TURQUOISE, GREY
8.	Tights	IVORY

ACCESSORIES FOR SPORT AND LEISURE   F

1.	Belt	GREY
2.	1 pair casual shoes	GREY
3.	1 pair walking shoes	NAVY
4.	1 pair earrings	YELLOW/GOLD
5.	Headscarf	GREY/YELLOW/BLACK/MULTI-COLOURED
6.	1 pair socks	GREY
7.	1 pair socks	NAVY
8.	Holdall	YELLOW/GREY

Create a Unique Wardrobe for You

You can use exactly the same formula as I did when planning a working wardrobe for Mary in planning a wardrobe for yourself. It would be wonderful if you could start completely afresh, and buy new clothes using all the colour, figure image and style knowledge you now possess. However, this is way beyond the finances of many of us; most will have to make do with what we've got, adding new items when we can afford them. A major part of creating a unique wardrobe is looking at what is there already with a very critical and knowledgeable eye and making the most of it. But it all becomes easy if you follow these steps:

1.   Fill in the Personal Profile form on page 126, adding your main and secondary colour characteristics, face shape, figure image and good and bad points.

2.   Fill in your lifestyle columns in order of priority.

3.   Turn back to your lifestyle category (pages 112 to 119) and select the suggested wardrobe under your main lifestyle first. This will need a minimum of twelve items of clothing, plus twelve accessories, and will be the mainstay of your wardrobe.

4.   Now decide which is your second lifestyle pattern and select a percentage of one of the wardrobes suggested, depending on the number of times you will need to use it.

5.   Using the same principle as above, work out the third, or leisure, part of your lifestyle.

6.   Choose your wardrobes and their colours and write them in your wardrobe organiser chart which follows on page 126. Use two main neutrals or colours which coordinate, and one or two coordinating accenting colours. From your 12 pieces, you will be able to get over 40 outfits for your main lifestyle. Also add colour which will coordinate in your alternative second and third lifestyles.

7.   Now, look into your own wardrobe. Once you have decided your best colours, your figure image and lifestyle, it's much easier to look in an unsentimental fashion at what is there. Place everything on the bed, jackets together, skirts together, blouses together etc. Put to one side everything you haven't worn in the past year: take to a dress agency (I call it trash for cash); or swap with your friends ('one woman's mistake is another's blessing' is a great truism). Try on all the clothes that are left. Do the colours and styles suit you? Can they be *adapted* to suit you? Are they appropriate for your lifestyle and compatible with one another? Are they in a good state of repair? Are they on your list of requirements?

   If all the answers are yes, place back in your wardrobe and tick off on your organiser. (If not, dispose of as above – you need to be ruthless.)

8.   Now look at your accessories in exactly the same way – shoes, stockings or tights, scarves, belts, etc. in individual piles. Are the shoes suitable and in the right colours? Are they in good condition? Do the scarves match and tone with your chosen colours (especially with the skirts, for a carefully chosen scarf colour can pull an outfit together)? Replace and tick off, or dispose of as above.

9.   Why not take advantage of this clean-out to organise your wardrobe in a much more logical and tidy way, using see-through organiser bags etc.

10.   Leave blank the items you do *not* have, and then you can take your wardrobe organiser with you when you go shopping inspired by your new-found confidence!

YOUR PERSONAL PROFILE

Name: . . . .

Main Colour Characteristic: . . . .
Second Colour Characteristic: . . . .
Face Shape: . . . .
Figure Image: . . . .
Figure Points to Emphasise: . . . .
Figure Points to Camouflage: . . . .
Height: . . . .
Weight: . . . .
Scale: . . . .

Lifestyle (list in order of priority) (A)... (B)... (C)... (D)... (E)... (F)...

Colour Psychology
RED – Exciting/Dangerous; BLUE – Calming/Cold
GREEN – Envy/Uplifting; YELLOW – Cheerful/Nauseating
ORANGE – Outgoing and Warm/Overpowering
PURPLE – Confusing/Regal; BLACK – Sophisticated/Dull

Brief Description of Lifestyle
Career: . . . .
. . . .
Social: . . . .
Hobbies: . . . .
Needs: . . . .

YOUR WARDROBE ORGANISER

Make a list of the items required for your lifestyle wardrobe below. Tick off those from your existing wardrobe which are right for your lifestyle, leaving gaps to be filled by clever shopping.

CAREER (A, B, C, D)	SOCIAL (E)	SPORT & LEISURE (F)
1.	1.	1. . . . .
2.	2.	2. . . . .
3.	3.	3. . . . .
4.	4.	4. . . . .
5.	5.	5. . . . .

6. . . . .   6. . . . .   6. . . . .

7. . . . .   7. . . . .   7. . . . .

8. . . . .   8. . . . .   8. . . . .

9. . . . .   9. . . . .   9. . . . .

10. . . . .   10. . . . .   10. . . . .

11. . . . .   11. . . . .   11. . . . .

12. . . . .   12. . . . .   12. . . . .

YOUR ACCESSORIES

Make a list of the accessories you will need to complete your looks, ticking off those you already have.

CAREER (A, B, C, D)	SOCIAL (E)	SPORT & LEISURE (F)
1.	1.	1. . . . .
2.	2.	2. . . . .
3.	3.	3. . . . .
4.	4.	4. . . . .
5.	5.	5. . . . .
6.	6.	6. . . . .
7.	7.	7. . . . .
8.	8.	8. . . . .
9.	9.	9. . . . .
10.	10.	10. . . . .
11.	11.	11. . . . .
12.	12.	12. . . . .

Shopping with Style

That outfit which always turns heads only does so because someone has spent time putting it together, and rehearsing it in front of a long mirror. It wasn't just thrown together. There is no success without effort!

Being a decisive dresser takes determination. Becoming confident about what suits you may take a little time and practice, but once you have studied your figure and all the styles and colours which will best suit you and your lifestyle, you will know all you need to about dressing with style. Make a list of the gaps on your wardrobe planner, then number them in order of priority. Always take this list with you when you go shopping and stick to it. This way you will be less likely to be pushed into making a mistake by an over-enthusiastic shop assistant, or a friend you have allowed to tag along. You should never ask for anyone else's advice: if you are not sure – don't buy. You know yourself better than anyone else, and only you know what your wardrobe needs are.

You may have already discovered that clothes sizes can be very misleading. One manufacturer's sizes can vary from another, but even more off-putting is that you can have the same manufacturer's range of clothing vary in size from one piece to another. For instance, you could find that their size 10 jacket is a perfect fit, but you need their size 12 skirt and size 14 blouse. This happened to me only this year, but all three together looked good, felt wonderful and coordinated with my existing wardrobe, so I bought them. Only use sizes as a guide and be prepared to try the other sizes to ensure a good fit.

Always look for clothes which will show off your best points and keep an eye out for designers who design for your figure image. When looking, take a pen and paper and make notes. Don't look at prices at this point, but for things you look good in. This is a learning exercise.

When trying on clothes, stand at a distance from the mirror so that you can check the balance from the front, side and back views. Start at the top and work your way down, asking yourself: is the colour good? Is the neckline the right shape for my face? Does it sit properly? How are the shoulders, are they big enough or too big? Does the blouse, jacket, or whatever hang correctly on me? How about the waistline; will it emphasise my good points and camouflage the bad ones?

Walk around and sit down in the outfit to check if it rides up, gapes, rubs or creases. What's the texture, pattern and fabric like for me? Will it go with the other items in my wardrobe?

After you think you have found what you are looking for, ask the shop assistant if you can take the goods home and return them if they are unsuitable. This will enable you to see how the items look with the rest of the clothes already hanging in your wardrobe. Most shops will agree to this if you keep the receipt.

A successful shopper perseveres because she knows what she is looking for, and she will usually get the shop assistant's cooperation. If an item in the shop isn't quite right in colour or size, ask the assistant to call another branch to see if they have what you want, enquire if they are getting more in, or if they can alter the one you have found to suit your figure image? A little money spent on personalising an outfit is well worth it, as you could otherwise spend a lot more on shoe leather and travel expenses searching for an alternative, not to mention time.

Travelling with Style

The secret of travelling with style is being prepared for any occasion. But you won't need a bulging suitcase. With a little organisation you should be able to achieve this from a small number of carefully selected items. This is how to do it. First, plot on paper the kind of itinerary you are expecting to encounter, then plan your wardrobe accordingly. For example, the following wardrobe is suitable for a one-week business and sight-seeing trip.

The most important rule is never pack any item that won't go with at least *two* other items in your suitcase. Never try to take too much.

1. Build from a basic coat/raincoat and jacket in your best neutral or basic colours which will tone with the rest of the clothes in your suitcase.

2. Add two skirts, making sure the jacket length and style look right with both skirts. A pleated style makes for a different look. The latter also makes a good travelling companion.

3. Add a pair of classic trousers cut for comfort as well as style (good in the same colour as your big coat or raincoat), for travelling, casual wear, sight-seeing and evening.

4. Add three coordinating blouses or shirts, at least one of which will take you from day to evening, plus a silk camisole or vest.

5. Pack two long-sleeved woollies – jumper/cardigans are the most versatile.

6. A two-piece silky dress is useful. The top can make one of your skirts or trousers look dressy, and the bottom can team up with the silk camisole/vest.

7. Add three pairs of shoes – pumps or smart sandals, classic court shoes and a sling-back court: the pumps for comfortable travel and sight-seeing, sling-backs or smart sandals for evening, and court shoes for business.

8. Have a leather shoulder bag for your money, passport, tickets, etc. An envelope bag in a neutral shade will take you from day to night, and this will fit into a briefcase.

9. Take with you your pearl earrings and necklace, your gold or silver chains and earrings.

10. Select three sets of underwear: one to wear, one in the wash, and one ready to wear. If you are travelling to a destination where it might be cold, add three thermal vests – they are a life saver without being bulky. Have six pairs of tights or stockings, to match hemline and shoe colour.

11. Don't forget toning belts and scarves in neutrals or accent colours – or your essential shoulder pads!

A FINAL WORD

You can't put a price on self-assurance and personal confidence – anything you can do which will bring inner confidence is worthwhile. I have written this book in the hope that it will help you and women everywhere discover the art of colour, style and confidence. I hope that this understanding of colour will change your life for the better – as it has done for me.

*I*ndex

SPECIAL READER
£10
DISCOUNT OFFER

Would you like to attend one of our Health and Image Weekends or a Colour and Style Day?

If so, please complete the coupon below for full details of all our courses and how to claim your special £10.00 discount.

Please mail to: Colour and Style File Ltd
                  FREEPOST 6
                  London W1E 1HR
                  (DO NOT AFFIX POSTAGE STAMPS IF POSTED IN GREAT BRITAIN, CHANNEL ISLANDS OR NORTHERN IRELAND)

- -

Rush me details of your Health & Image Weekends
and Colour and Style Days

Name: ....

Address: ....

....

....

Phone No: ....

PERSONALISE YOUR *COLOUR AND STYLE FILE* WITH THIS SPECIAL READER OFFER!

We are offering readers a leather-look COLOUR AND STYLE ORGANISER (handbag-size) at the special discount price of £15.95 (normally £25.95). The organiser will be personalised to your requirements, containing fabric samples of your best colours and information on how to co-ordinate them successfully. We will also include a wardrobe planner designed for your lifestyle and figure image together with your own computer profile. Just fill in the details below and send to us at the address given on this page:

Name .... Phone No ....

Address ....

....

....

Main colour characteristic .... Second colour characteristic ....

Face shape .... Body shape ....

Figure points to emphasise ....

Figure points to camouflage ....

Height .... Weight .... Shoe size ....

Please tick the appropriate box   Figure image 1 ☐ 2 ☐ 3 ☐ 4 ☐ 5 ☐ 6 ☐

Bone structure (scale) Fine ☐ Medium ☐ Large ☐

Career profile – Pick 3 of the following 6 and list in order of priority

(A) ...... (B) ...... (C) ...... (D) ...... (E) ...... (F) ......

What comes into your mind when you think of the following colours?

Tick the appropriate box

RED: Exciting ☐ Dangerous ☐   BLUE: Calming ☐ Cold ☐

GREEN   Superstitious ☐ Uplifting ☐   YELLOW: Cheerful ☐ Overpowering ☐

ORANGE: Outgoing ☐ Overpowering ☐   PURPLE: Confusing ☐ Regal ☐

BLACK: Sophisticated ☐ Deathly ☐

I enclose a cheque for £ .... or debit my credit card as follows:

Access ☐   Visa ☐   Card Number ☐☐☐☐☐☐☐☐☐☐☐☐☐☐☐☐

Expiry Date: ....

Signature for credit card transactions ....

Please mail to: Colour and Style File Ltd
                 FREEPOST 6
                 London W1E 1HR

(DO NOT AFFIX POSTAGE STAMPS IF POSTED IN GREAT BRITAIN, CHANNEL ISLANDS OR NORTHERN IRELAND).

If you do not wish to remove this page, please copy your answers onto a separate sheet of paper.